SPIRITUAL
BOOT CAMP

SPIRITUAL
BOOT CAMP

(A Mental Workout)

16 Weeks to Mental Muscle

By

James J. Mellon

For my Family –
Kevin, Nora and Will

CONTENTS

Spiritual
Boot Camp

(A Mental Workout)

16 Weeks to Mental Muscle

So, one day I was driving to the gym and a thought hit me. If I spent as much time on my Spiritual Practice as I do on my body, things would really change. Right then, I passed a group of people in the park being put through their paces. Some guy was yelling at them to FALL DOWN, STAND UP, JUMP, KNEES TO YOUR CHEST, ON YOUR BACK... I was at a red light and I was breaking a sweat just listening to him. "Wow," I thought, "what if I had some guy in my mind who constantly kept me on track, wouldn't let me slack off, made me stop complaining, never took "no" for an answer, always held me to what I SAID I WANTED TO DO. What would THAT be like?"

What if I created a Boot Camp for the mind? What if I policed my mental capacity for creativity on a daily basis? What if I built strength and resistance to be able to lift myself above any perceived obstacle? What if I spent as much time on my INNER life as I do on my OUTER life? What if?

WHAT IF?

From those two words came the idea of Spiritual Boot Camp. I knew that I had to create this thing. I had no idea what it would be, other than POWERFUL. And that was enough.

I announced it in church the next Sunday. As the Founding Pastor of a New Thought church in Los Angeles, I knew there would be others who felt as I did. I asked for ten people to take this journey with me. A journey of Truth! This was not for the faint of heart. I would require commitment - commitment to the Self. This wasn't going to be something you could try and see if you liked it or not. If you didn't like it, TOUGH! You signed up, now you have to finish it. After all, it is BOOT CAMP!

I was pretty amazed when the first Boot Camp was filled within minutes of my announcement. In fact, there was a waiting list. To date I have facilitated four 16-week Boot Camps, and the next one is filled and raring to go. Clearly, this was an idea whose time had come. Now it was time for me to get in there and figure it out. The following pages will illustrate what has come from the first four rounds of Boot Camp. I am sure there is more to know, more to be, more to explore and more to sweat out. But I'll tell you one thing I **ABSOLUTELY KNOW,** if you follow this sixteen-week Boot Camp, you will never be the same again.

The following pages will guide you through Spiritual Boot Camp. It is a sixteen-week transformative experience that will pump you up, turn you inside out and strengthen you in such a way that Life will become what it was always meant to be - AWESOME! They say that knowledge is power. What they say is correct. But unless you are ready to take that knowledge and put it to use, what good is it really?

If you're ready to take your life in a new direction, if you're ready to take control of your mind and create a tomorrow that seems out of reach, if you're ready to put some MENTAL SWEAT into your Spiritual/Mental creative muscle, then this is for you.

Make the commitment! Take the challenge! Strengthen your Mental Muscle! TURN THE PAGE, literally!

What is Spiritual Boot Camp?

A journey to the Truth. Not anyone else's truth, but your Truth. There is something within that drives you forward, pushes you to reach out and stretch your imagination. Every desire you've ever had, every dream you've ever contemplated, and every future you've ever stepped into, was backed by a Force within your mind. It all begins with YOU. The question is, do you recognize yourself within your own life?

In Spiritual Boot Camp, you are asked to go fearlessly into the mind and seek out the origins of your individual personality. Why do I react this way? Why do I always do this or that? What is my intention? Do I believe in what I say? Can I make a decision and stick to it? What are my beliefs? How are those beliefs running my life? Can I? Will I? Dare I?

YES! You can! You will! And Dare Away!

"What mind can conceive, man can achieve!"
Ralph Waldo Emerson

Spiritual Boot Camp is designed to bring you face-to- face with yourself. It is not a series of laws or tips on ways to get rich, make more friends, find your perfect life partner or any of those things most books are promising these days. This is a regimen of honest, rigorous self-study. Everything you need is right where you are. It's not outside of you. It is not something to reach for out there. It is something you discover within. You just have to be willing to go there. Once you get an idea of who you are, and how you operate in the world, you can start deciding who you want to be and how you want to live.

It's YOUR CHOICE, not anyone else's. That's the first thing to realize.

YOU ARE AT CHOICE! YOU DECIDE!

But first, you have to GET DIRTY!

One day at Boot Camp, one of the group shared that he felt "as if all of my life I've been walking around in a white suit that I was afraid to get dirty." So I said, "It's time we all got dirty!" Enough of the Sunday clothes! We needed clothes we could muddy up. We needed bodies that weren't afraid to fall down, skin our knees and come up laughing. We needed to LIVE LIFE TO THE FULLEST. FEARLESS! EXPECTANT! JOYOUS!

"Our greatest glory is not in never failing, but in rising every time we fall."
Confucius

In other words, don't be afraid to fall down. Sometimes it's the hardest fall that gives us the deepest perspective. But enough speculation – it's all theory until you actually DO IT.

SO LET'S DO IT!

Pre-Training

The Life Force in you is bursting at the seams, waiting for you to open the floodgates and let IT out. But, before we get started, there are three directives that you must begin to work. They are as follows:

RELEASE

LET GO

ALLOW

RELEASE any and all preconceived ideas you have of yourself. I don't care if you have never succeeded at anything in your entire life, it doesn't matter. Release what you think you know, and start every day with the mantra: I know nothing, now what can I learn? You are then starting from a position of power.

LET GO of the past. Good, bad or indifferent, the past is something that has passed you by. Nothing can stop you quicker than if you spend your time looking back. You have arrived at this particular moment in time and whatever got you here is not as important as what is going to propel you into your future. And it doesn't have to be your past that dictates your future. It is the PRESENT. So, give yourself a present and let go of the past.

ALLOW the passionate energy of Life within you to take over. Allow yourself to know yourself. Allow yourself to reintroduce yourself to your life. Allow something bigger than you to become the guiding Force of your life.

RELEASE - LET GO - ALLOW

It truly doesn't matter what your Spiritual Practice is. This is not about religion. It's about YOU. It's about the place you hold in whatever understanding you have of God. Regardless of what has come before, you are at the threshold of what will follow from this moment on. By using the following exploration of Truth, you can choreograph the most exquisite dance of Life you could ever imagine. And if you don't dance, just jump around a bit. If I've learned anything from Boot Camp, it's that I cannot and will no longer define myself as someone who does or doesn't do anything. I am limitless potential!

Life is waiting for YOU to HAPPEN! Don't wait for IT!

Get dirty! Get to know yourself.

If not now, **WHEN**?

The Boot Camp Program

It's simple, really. You show up in your own life, do the work necessary to know the Truth about who you are, and make changes based on what you now know. The first step is to SHOW UP.

The program is a twice weekly, one-hour session (one-on-one with the book, or a group of people doing the Boot Camp together). Each week, you will follow a specific regimen designated to create a firm, rooted Spiritual/ Mental practice.

Note: When I facilitate my Boot Camps, I sit in a circle with ten to twelve participants and we go over each directive and what it means. There are notes throughout the book for group participation. If you are facilitating, your only job is to listen and *allow* the session to play itself out. Be very careful not to turn it into a group therapy session.

"The life which is unexamined is not worth living."
Plato

Repeat to yourself: **TODAY, I DECIDE TO LIVE FULLY!**

Today is about the decision to take your life into your hands and make it your own. Success, prosperity, love, creativity, self-expression - it's an open door to wherever you decide to go. No one other than YOU will make the difference. And that, I promise you, is **GOOD NEWS!**

The Five Building Blocks

Meditation

Communication

Intention

Attention

Accountability

These five directives will be the foundation for all you will achieve in the next sixteen weeks. They are your tools! They are your drills! They are the way to Freedom.

Here's how it works:

Twice a week, you will dedicate a one-hour block of time to the program. Make sure you schedule two or three days between your sessions to enable you to accomplish the work. Whether you do it alone or with a group, it is imperative that you stick to your schedule for the entire sixteen-week course. Remember, this is a commitment to yourself and you owe it to YOU to succeed, no one else.

Meditation

At the start of each session, begin with ten minutes of

Meditation. And before you start squirming at the thought of sitting in a lotus position, all "pretzeled up" and uncomfortable, let me say that meditation is a personal thing. The purpose of it is to calm your mind, to quiet the voices, to hear the only voice worth hearing, your higher Self.

So, whatever it takes to accomplish that directive, that will be your meditation. In my Boot Camp, we have soothing music, candlelight and a quiet atmosphere. People must be in their seats by 7:30 a.m. each morning and, for ten minutes, we sit quietly. Some people keep their eyes open, others close them. Occasionally, one of us will lie on the floor, or stand and stretch. Once, one of our Boot Campers got so relaxed that he fell off the chair and landed on the floor – luckily, it was carpeted.

However it works for you - that is your directive. Find a way to quiet the world around you and prepare for the rest of the hour. You will be provided with a quote which you can choose to take into your meditation.

Communication

Following the ten-minute meditation comes **Communication**. If you are doing this alone, you will take this time to write about what is going on in your life. Journaling is a vibrant part of our Boot Camp and helps extract thoughts/beliefs that are caught in the sub-conscious layer of our overall consciousness. Pages have been provided for you at the end of each chapter. As you journal, remember to keep focused on whatever the directive is for that week. Just keep it real! Don't write about flowers, if that's not your experience. If you're in hell, write about the flames.

If you are doing this in a group, each of the group takes an agreed-upon amount of time to communicate what is going on with them. Keep it to a minimum and don't allow yourself to go off on tangents that do not concern the directive. Remember, we are about the business of directing our thoughts to a constructive place of transformation. That doesn't mean filtering your life through rose-colored glasses. Tell the facts as they are, but leave the drama behind. There is absolutely NO cross-talk. Cross-talk is the way we usually communicate in modern day society. We interject in the middle of sentences and express our agreement or objection before a statement is finished. We find the need to give our opinion before the originating opinion has been finalized. This causes the person speaking to veer off their point. It stops the natural flow of the thought process. Respect one another and allow for the authentic voice to have its say.

Intention

Next is the weekly **Intention**. This is the global directive for the week. Each week, you will have a specific intention on which to focus. These intentions are designed to reveal your personal belief system. As you stay conscious of your intention, you will watch as this intention plays itself out in your everyday affairs. You will be amazed at how little you realize what is going through your mind on a day-by-day basis. Your beliefs are directing your thoughts, which are creating your experience, even as you sit reading this sentence. Now THAT is exciting news. That's something to look at!

Attention

This brings us to the next directive - **Attention**. Wherever we put our attention creates an energy that manifests on another level in proportion to our ability to attend to our thoughts. This is the Law of Cause and Effect.

If you continually put your attention on how much you don't have, you continue to find situations where you don't have. If, conversely, you put your attention on what you do have, and how thankful you are for having it, then you will find situations where you will manifest more. It really is that simple. Paying attention to your thoughts is the most rigorous part of Boot Camp. However, with diligent attention, you can profoundly change the course of your life.

Accountability

Once you start the road to freedom, building your mental muscle, enriching and strengthening your Spiritual life, it is imperative that you follow the most important directive of Boot Camp - **Accountability**. From the Latin *accomptare* (to account), accountability is your promise to yourself to account for your actions, decisions and results. Dan Zedra, author of the best selling book, Think Big, writes this about accountability:

> *"Some favorite expressions of small children: It's not my fault. . . They made me do it. . . I forgot. Some favorite expressions of adults: It's not my job. . . No one told me. . . It couldn't be helped. True freedom begins and ends with personal accountability."*

I thought this quote was appropriate, given some of the excuses I have heard in Boot Camp over the past year and a half. The most common obstacle to self-awareness, and subsequently to personal responsibility, is the notion that something is out of your control. This is not true. While it is true that you cannot change another person or rewrite history, you are always in the power seat in your own life. You have the power to **react** in whatever way you decide to react. You may not be able to change what has happened but you can certainly change how you **react** to the situation. That is personal Power.

Spiritual Boot Camp is here to help you recover that Power!

Repeat to yourself: **TODAY, I DECIDE TO LIVE FULLY!**

I would like to suggest that you do not read the rest of this book in advance of doing the work. Each week is designed to focus your mind on a given Intention. We are seeking clarity, understanding and intuition. There is plenty of "noise" in this world to pollute the mind and keep it so occupied that it doesn't have the capacity to consciously create. Oh, we're creating. We're always creating. But deliberate, conscious thinking is far more powerful than reactive thinking.

Take each week and work it. Keep your mind focused on the Intention at hand and the tasks you will be asked to do. *Allow* yourself to experience the anticipation of success. See yourself at the end of this journey replenished, revitalized, reborn. *Release* the past and create the future. It all begins in this present moment. *Let Go* of anything that could hold you back. There is nowhere to go but forward - forward with *Confidence*!

"If one advances confidently in the direction of his dreams, and endeavors to live the life which he has imagined, he will meet with a success unexpected in common hours."
Henry David Thoreau

Welcome to Day One of Spiritual Boot Camp

WEEK ONE

YOUR WORD

.

WEEK ONE

Day One

Meditation: (Ten minute minimum)

Take the following quote with you into your meditation. Allow your mind to release all unwanted thoughts and consider these words.

"I like to think of enlightenment as a never-ending horizon. You get close to it and then another horizon shows up."
Deepak Chopra

Communication: What thoughts came up during your meditation? Were you able to relax and let go? How in control of your own mind are you? As you begin Spiritual Boot Camp, allow yourself to stay completely open to what flows through your mind.

- Write your thoughts, without judgment, on the blank pages provided at the end of each week. You do not need to be brilliant, only honest. Make an honest assessment of where you are. Put it down in words for reference later.

- If you are in a group, share your thoughts. Keep mindful of a time allotment. Do not cross talk. Opinions are useless. We are about the business of revealing Truth, which is personal to each of us. Allow yourself to listen, and reflect on how it relates to you.

Intention: This week's Intention/Directive is *Your Word.*

Today you will choose a word that will become your intention for the entire sixteen-week Boot Camp. Everyone has a *Word* within them. Something that is pressing against your conscious mind with such force and passion that it almost aches to be released. It can be quite subtle in its desire to be known, or it can be a brass band marching through the parade that is your mind. Either way, it's there.

Your *Word* can be an inner longing, a forgotten dream, a deep desire. It is the reason you're taking this Boot Camp. It is what you want most. You might not even be conscious of what that is in this present moment. Not a problem. There is something within you that knows.

- If you are doing this on your own, take a moment here and "listen" to your thoughts. Ask yourself:

What do I want?

- Group: Each person gets a moment to reflect on their reason for taking this Boot Camp. What word follows?

Chances are you have already thought of your *Word*. Very often, it has a way of choosing us. This happens when Divine Intuition steps in and aligns us with our highest good. Frequently, in Boot Camp, it comes as soon as I suggest it. And sometimes it takes awhile. Again, don't worry about it. You might have to listen a bit to find the word that fits. Not a problem. Your *Word* is already etched in your True Being. Just *allow* it to come forward.

Some *Words* revealed in Boot Camp:

Commitment
Release
Believe
Authentic
Faith
Flow
Now
Peace
Defenselessness
Detachment
Purification
Felicity
Focus
Expand
Be
Discover
Impeccability
Connection
Love

Each of these *Words* represents a personal journey - a commitment to knowing more, revealing more, understanding more. Whatever your word may be, it is backed by a determination to explore its meaning in your life. There is nothing more important than <u>your</u> life. Starting today, there is nothing more important than *Your Word*.

Other than to fellow Boot Campers, I would suggest that you keep *Your Word* to yourself. Remember, we are working with a Law. What we put into it comes out exactly as we believe. No one's opinion matters but your own. So, *allow* your thoughts to be just that, your thoughts.

Attention: How we pay attention to our intentions determines how and if they will materialize in our lives. Making the decision to do something, without the act of actually "doing it" is what keeps most people sitting in front of their television sets living other people's lives. The following is a list of directives that will give you the opportunity to "activate" your intention.

Directives for the Week:

1. Each morning, when you wake up, before you do anything or say anything to anyone, write your initial thoughts in the blank journal pages. Again, they don't have to be brilliant, they just have to be honest.

2. Work with your word throughout the week. Make a conscious decision to remember *Your Word* at least three times throughout each day.

3. Before going to bed, in that moment right before you close your eyes and drift into dreamland, remind yourself of *Your Word*.

Remember: What you tell yourself is far more important than what others tell you.

Keep Your Word!

WEEK ONE

Day Two

Meditation: Bring *Your Word* into your meditation.

> *"Self-trust is the first secret of success."*
> *Ralph Waldo Emerson*

Begin to trust your inner "knower." There is something within you, call it Divine Intuition, that is readily available at all times. Put it to work for you! *Allow* it to inform you of your highest good.

Communication: What has come up since you found *Your Word*? Does it feel like the right word? Have you had an urge to change it? Are you having trouble owning it? Do you believe (I mean, really believe) that it is attainable, whatever it is? How has it begun to play out in your everyday life?

- Write down your answers to these questions and whatever else is going through your mind with reference to your word. Use the blank pages provided at the end of the chapter.

It's always amazing to me when someone in the group chooses a word, and just the choice alone causes this atomic reaction to take place in their life. On my last Boot Camp I chose the word "detachment." I can't tell you how many things I suddenly realized I needed to detach from. It just works that way. You make a decision, commit to an intention, pay attention to it and next thing you know, you're actually succeeding at what you set out to do. What a concept! My thought really does create my experience.

- If you are in a group, share your thoughts with
  one another regarding your word. Keep
  mindful of a time allotment. No cross-talk.

Remember: It's okay to change your word throughout the
week. Just commit to having one firmly in place before
week two.

Accountability: Make an inventory of the directives and
how well you accomplished them.

1. Did you pay *Attention* to *Your Word?*

2. Did you write each morning?

3. Did you take three conscious moments to be
   mindful of *Your Word?*

4. Did you bring *Your Word* to mind before going to
   sleep?

If not, why not?

Don't be afraid to be brutally honest with your answers. It
is only by acknowledging the facts and owning up to your
own "story" that you can begin to rewrite it.

Quotes from Boot Camp

*"My word is Acceptance. I don't know why that came to
me but I realized this week that in my world, as a child,
everything had to be perfect or else I wasn't safe.
Accepting things as they are is hard for me. So I think I'll*

stick with Acceptance."

"Faith! Something is telling me to focus my attention on Faith. I feel like I carry the world on my shoulders and I'm ready to let God start carrying it. In fact, He/She, Father/Mother God, Whoever can carry me as well."

"The word 'Authentic' came to me right away. I don't know what my life is supposed to be or what I'm supposed to be doing with it, but I have a feeling that there is an 'Authenticity' that doesn't need to be found, it needs to be uncovered. And I am SOOOOOO ready to uncover it."

"When I heard the word 'Felicity' come into my head I didn't know what it meant. That was weird. So I looked it up. It means 'Intense Happiness.' That works for me. I'll stick with Felicity."

Continue with this week's directives!

Keep Your Word!

YOUR WORD

_____

_____

_____

_____

_____

_____

_____

_____

_____

_____

_____

_____

_____

_____

_____

_____

_____

_____

_____

_____

_____

_____

_____

_____

_____

_____

YOUR WORD

WEEK TWO

NO COMPLAINING

WEEK TWO

Day One

Meditation: (Ten minute minimum)

With one week's work behind you, bring **Your Word** into your meditation and allow your mind to focus on the energy surrounding the **Word.** You have begun to create an "Energy Circle" around your life. Let yourself feel this energy.

> *"Empty yourself of everything. Let the mind rest at peace."*
> *The Tao Te Ching*

Communication: How does this meditation differ from the first two? Can you begin to feel an "Energy" surrounding you? What did **Your Word** bring to your world this week?

- Write your thoughts, without judgment, on the blank pages provided. Don't compete with yourself or anyone else for the most profound perceptions. Just tell it like it is.

- If you are in a group, share your thoughts. Keep mindful of a time allotment. No cross-talking. Opinions are useless. We are revealing Truth. Listen and you will hear it.

- Note: If, for some reason, you feel that **Your Word** needs to be changed, go for it. It's your decision. Just allow yourself to listen to your Divine Intuition. You'll know exactly what to do. Don't allow yourself to get frustrated. Trust yourself.

Intention: This week's Intention/Directive is **No Complaining.**

Have you ever noticed how much complaining goes on in the world? Perhaps you take part in this phenomenon. Complaining is something we do when we are actively avoiding the situation. The energy we put into complaining creates the "illusion" that we are actually doing something constructive. We're not! Let's make no mistake about it.

When we complain, we are just reinforcing the issue even further into the black whole of hopelessness.

Many times in Boot Camp people will fight for their right to complain. "It helps me realize what's bothering me." "It's a way to let off steam." One woman told the group that, as a Jewish woman, "complaining was considered an Olympic sport." I told her that, by growing up in an Irish Catholic household, I couldn't imagine any other nationality holding the "gold" on complaining.

Regardless of your reasons, complaining is a waste of time. You cannot live life to the fullest when you are focusing on what is wrong. That doesn't mean that we don't acknowledge the problem. We do. But we focus our attention on the Truth of the situation, which is to know that behind the problem is the solution.

This week, you will NOT COMPLAIN about anything!

Sound impossible? It's not. It's actually quite freeing. The first time I gave this Intention, I was surrounded by students for the entire week and each time I started to complain about something (there truly is not delineation between teacher and student), one of my students would raise an eyebrow or smile in just "that way" that I would understand. Don't go there!

The most important thing to remember about complaining is this:

Complaining is a CHOICE!

Attention: Paying attention to something like complaining is an interesting thing. Most of us aren't aware of how much complaining we actually do. You may find that you don't really complain that much. Or you might find that you are one of the finalists at the Olympics. Regardless of how much you participate, the process is illuminating. The most important thing is for you to pay ***Attention*** to your complaining.

Directives for the Week: Continue journaling each morning.

Each time you find yourself complaining, or catch yourself about to complain, ask yourself these questions:

1. When do I complain?

2. Why do I complain?

3. What am I avoiding in this moment?

Behind each complaint is something that needs to be known. It's very difficult to hear when the noise level of complaining is so high. Quieting the mind from the complaint allows us to know the Truth in any situation. So, as you still the complaint, replace it with the Truth (the higher thought).

This week, along with your morning journaling, just before you go to bed, write out how your day went with regard to complaining.

- How did I do?

- Did I pay attention to my complaining?

- Did I recognize what was behind the complaint?

- Did I replace the complaint with the Truth?

- Am I willing to do better tomorrow?

Remember: Today's Intention is tomorrow's success.

No Complaining!

WEEK TWO

Day Two

Meditation: Bring Your Word into your meditation.

*"Happiness is the meaning and the purpose of life,
the whole aim and end of human existence."*
Aristotle

Communication: How does it feel to live without complaining? Are you good at it? Are you surprised by the amount of complaining you do? Is it less than you expected, more? When you reflect on what you've written in your journal, what do you think about yourself? What's behind the complaining? Do you know? If not, keep listening.

- Write your thoughts to these questions, and whatever else has come up for you in this moment, on the blank pages provided.

- If you are in a group, share your thoughts. Keep mindful of a time allotment. No cross-talk. Learn to listen without responding.

Accountability: Make an inventory of the directives and how well you accomplished them.

1. Did you write each morning?

2. Did you really pay ATTENTION to your complaining by asking the questions provided whenever you caught yourself "in the act?"

3. Did you conclude each day with an assessment of how you did?

If not, why not?

Keep on yourself as you go through this process. Notice whether or not you keep promises you make to yourself. If we lack the respect to follow through on what we intend, it is something to reflect on.

This is what is meant by Self-Respect!

Quotes from Boot Camp

"This is really frustrating. I thought I was someone who didn't complain much. I guess it's all relative to what you think of as 'much.' Now it feels like even a little is too much."

"I don't know about the rest of you but the gold medal is mine."

"I know one thing. Something has to give because I can't keep doing it this way. I'm just gonna put my complaints under my pillow and let the pillow fairy handle it."

"What do you do when you realize that all of your friends are complainers? I like my energy circle but I don't want to be in there alone."

"I've noticed that there's always a chain reaction when I complain."

"Sometimes I feel like I go from kvetch to kvetch, crisis to crisis. This no complaining thing is exhausting."

"I realized that 'My Story' is just one big complaint!"

"I guess on one level, there really isn't anything to complain about."

Continue with this week's directives!

No Complaining!

NO COMPLAINING

NO COMPLAINING

WEEK THREE

EXPECTATIONS

WEEK THREE

Day One

Meditation: (Ten minute minimum)

Clearing your life of complaining has allowed you to build on your Energy Circle. Knowing the Truth, rather than focusing solely on the facts, is a way of life that transcends chaos and brings harmony. It allows for Inner Peace. Bring these words into your meditation.

> *"In Truth, to attain to interior peace, one must*
> *be willing to pass through the contrary*
> *to peace."*
> Swami Brahmananda

Communication: How has not complaining changed your life? Has it? Are you willing to continue this until it becomes second nature? If not, why? Does it feel natural to complain or is it starting to feel natural NOT to complain. Do you hear the complaint when it's internal and perhaps not spoken? Those are deadly.

One Boot Camper put it this way: "I don't have to take things personally, but I also don't have to take things as they are."

Eliminating the complaint allows us to see things clearly and make the choice to change what we don't like, what isn't useful, what doesn't serve us, into something that brings joy, is beneficial and serves our higher good.

- Take a look at your journal, focusing on what you wrote each night during your week of no complaining. Write a paragraph or two explaining what you experienced, learned and decided based on your work. You can use the blank pages provided at the end of this week's work.

- If you are in a group, share your thoughts. Keep mindful of a time allotment. No cross-talk.

- In answer to the person who asked what to do when all of your friends seem to be complainers, you will find that as you stop complaining, others around you will follow suit. It's hard to complain when there's no one to complain to. And if that doesn't work, you will most likely find a new group of friends.

Intention: This week's Intention/Directive is **Expectancy**.

Believe it or not, you are expecting something to happen in your life right now in this very moment. All of us have expectations that are either buried, unconscious or rote. Add this to our conscious expectations and you have the motor that fuels our forward momentum.

EXPECTATIONS

"We must learn to reawaken and keep ourselves awake, not by mechanical aid, but by an infinite expectation of the dawn."
Henry David Thoreau

As Thoreau so eloquently puts it, we must always expect the dawn of a new idea, a new thought, and a new realization. When you go to sleep at night, don't you expect to wake to another day? If you don't, take a look at that. We all expect the sun to rise on the next morning. So why is it that we have to work so hard to expect the Truth to come forth in the midst of a dark reality? This difficulty is something we have learned. And we can re-learn it! We can refocus our expectations to create richer, fuller and more successful lives.

When I expect something to happen, truly expect it, IT HAPPENS!

Expect the Good! What's the alternative?

During one session, it became clear that most people confuse expectation with hope. Hope is good - it's better than despair. But it's not strong enough to create what you want. Expectancy leaves no room for failure. Hope depends on others. Expectancy realizes that you are a co-creator with the Creator - however you define the Creator in your personal relationship with Source.

This week you will focus on EXPECTANCY!

Get in touch with what you actually are expecting right at this moment. Are you expecting to have a great week? Are you expecting to win the lottery? Do you expect things to get better? Do you expect this Boot Camp to be a changing force in your life? What are you expecting? It's important for you to know the answer to that question as it relates to all areas of your life.

I expect only that which is GOOD!

Attention: In every situation there is an expectancy. Most of the time it is unspoken, but it's there. Your job this week is to continually check in with yourself and see what the expectation is. Will dinner with so-and-so be boring or fun? Will this job interview turn into something or will it be like all the others? What are you expecting it to be? That's what it will be. Pay *Attention* and you will see how you are creating your experience through your expectations.

Directives for the Week: Pay *Attention* to what you are expecting.

When you wake up, take a moment and see what you are expecting for your day. Write it down. Then ask yourself the following questions:

1. Am I being honest with myself?

2. Is this what I wish to experience?

3. What would be the most productive expectation for my day?

Remember: There is no limit to what you can expect. Only you can limit yourself. And, if you read this and hear this voice inside your head saying "My life is limited and there's nothing I can do about it," tell yourself ENOUGH!

The only reason your life is limited is because that is what you are expecting. You were probably taught to expect that.

I can clearly hear my mother telling me, "Don't expect too much and you won't be disappointed." She meant well and I know she was trying to protect me. After all, I wanted to be a Broadway star. And, as my grandmother used to say, "There's a lot of rejection in the acting world." Clearly, my mother got it from her mother and hers before her. Looking back, I wondered how any of them knew about the rejection of actors. None of them were in the "business."

Just so you know, I starred in my first Broadway show when I was twenty-five. Clearly, I expected it!

This week, along with your morning journaling, before you go to bed, write out how your day went with regard to expectancy.

- Did what I expected play out? If not, what changed?

- Did I pay attention to what I was expecting in each interaction?

- Am I beginning to expose expectations that are old and useless? If yes, make a list.

- Are my expectations my own, or are they handed down from the past?

I expect only that which is GOOD!

WEEK THREE

Day Two

Meditation: As you enter meditation this day, bring with you an expectancy of knowing more, allowing more, hearing more. Instruct your mind to release any unwanted thoughts, ideas or images. Then drift into the "silence" to commune with your True Self.

> *"In the attitude of silence the soul finds the path in a clearer light,*
> *and what is elusive and deceptive resolves itself into crystal clearness."*
> *Mahatma Gandhi*

Communication: Thinking back to the start of this week, how did you expect it to go? Did it live up to your expectations? Were you able to re-direct specific expectations to bring about a more desirable result? Were you surprised at what types of expectations you already had in place? Did you notice how you reacted to others' expectations of you?

- Being as clear and honest as possible, let yourself speak aloud your thoughts from the past couple of days. You can read what you wrote each night as a prelude and then continue by allowing your thoughts to pour out at random - this is not a performance, but a releasing. Now jot down whatever sticks out in your mind about what you just said on the blank pages provided.

- If you are in a group, share your thoughts. Keep mindful of a time allotment. No cross-talk. Allow your mind to release whatever thoughts you have about the directive. Be brutally honest.

Accountability: Make an inventory of the directives and how well you accomplished them.

1. Did you write each morning?

2. Did you pay *ATTENTION* to what you were expecting in any given situation?

3. Did you conclude each day with an assessment of how you did?

If not, why not?

By now, you have a pretty clear indication of what to expect with regard to Boot Camp. If you are one of those people who start out strong and then lose interest or peter out at the finish line, *EXPECT MORE OF YOURSELF*! No one is going to step up to the plate and pitch for you. If you expect success, you have to do what it takes to succeed.

Remember: **You** are the only one who can make a difference in your life! There may be others who inspire, but you alone will either make use of or toss aside what they have to offer. It's all up to **you**.

EXPECTATIONS

This is what is meant by Self-Reliant!

<u>Quotes from Boot Camp</u>

"Yesterday I realized that I don't expect much from my life considering who I am. When I heard this in my head I thought, WHAT? Actually I thought something else, but I'm being polite."

"Someone once told me, 'Hope for the best, prepare for the worst.' I don't remember who it was, but I'm pissed off because that's how I live my life."

"I've noticed that my life is about 'extremes.' I expect the highs, and therefore I expect the lows. And that's exactly what I get, the highs and the lows."

"There's been an umbrella in my car for many years...on many levels. I guess I'm expecting a lot of rain, literally and figuratively."

Continue with this week's directives!

Expectancy: "My success is non-negotiable!"

EXPECTATIONS

_____

_____

_____

_____

_____

_____

_____

_____

_____

_____

_____

_____

_____

_____

_____

_____

_____

_____

_____

_____

_____

_____

_____

_____

EXPECTATIONS

_____

_____

_____

_____

_____

_____

_____

_____

_____

_____

_____

_____

_____

_____

_____

_____

_____

_____

_____

_____

_____

_____

_____

_____

WEEK FOUR

BELIEF

WEEK FOUR

Day One

Meditation: (Ten minute minimum)

I expect only GOOD!

Use this sentence to focus your Intention as you Meditate.

Communication: Last week, you were asked to allow yourself a free flow of thought regarding your expectations of life. Letting our thoughts fly from our consciousness into the ethers of audible sound is a freeing experience (if we give ourselves over to it). How did it feel for you?

The overall directive was to take our waking thoughts and discover what we were expecting for the day. If we didn't like what we were expecting, we were directed to change the expectation. How did that go? Did it come easy? Are your expectations accessible and clear? Are there expectations, core expectations, which have control of your day-to-day existence? Does it change things when you decide to expect only the GOOD?

- Looking back over this week, re-reading your nightly journaling and exploring the seven-day journey, write down your perceptions on the blank pages provided.

- Make a special effort to uncover expectations that are placed upon you from outside of yourself.

- If you are in a group, share your thoughts. Keep mindful of a time allotment. No cross-talk, but keep notes on what resonates with you.

Intention: This week's Intention/Directive is **_Belief._**

I remember sitting on the floor of our living room, one Easter, watching Mary Martin fly across our modern black-and-white television screen as Peter Pan. (Does it even seem possible that there was actually black-and-white television in our lifetime?) At one point, she looked out from her captive box and asked us to say: "I do believe in fairies." This was so that Tinkerbell would live. And, I can tell you that it never crossed my mind to not believe in fairies. Cynicism would come much later.

Just yesterday, my eight-year old son announced that he no longer believed in the Easter Bunny. He said he knew it was just a guy dressed up in a bunny costume. For him, it no longer made any sense. So I asked him about Santa Claus and he looked me straight in the eyes and said, "Dad, of course there's a Santa Claus, I'm not that stupid." I was relieved.

Behind every expectation is the belief that it will or will not happen. If you have found it difficult to direct your expectations, that's because your belief system isn't creating the foundation for this new expectation. If you believe something will happen, you then expect it to happen and it happens! It's the belief that informs the thought that informs the expectancy. Let me repeat that.

Belief informs the Thought that informs the Expectancy.

We each have a set of beliefs that we use as we navigate life. There was a time when the belief, that the world was flat, kept mankind from going too far in any one direction for fear of falling off the Earth. Actually, I think we still have that belief somewhere imbedded in our collective consciousness. We somehow believe in failure, so we are conscious not to make our endeavors too vast. We believe that there's not enough money in the world for everyone, so we stick to a "fixed income" that is safe. We believe that we can be hurt if we love too deeply, so we keep our affections on the surface, protecting our intimate feelings. We believe a lot of things that keep us from falling off the Earth. But we are made of Heaven, not Earth.

> *"Our deepest fear is not that we are inadequate.*
> *Our deepest fear is that we are powerful beyond measure."*
> *Marianne Williamson*

What do you believe about yourself? When you look in the mirror, who do you see? If you look around at your life, what you have accomplished, what you have created, your successes, your failures, your relationships, you will find tangible proof for what you have believed up to this point.

Whether or not you like what you see doesn't matter. The great news is that you can change your beliefs, change your thinking and create new expectancy. What you are looking at, in this moment, does not have to be what you see tomorrow, or even in the next moment.

One Boot Camper said: "I liken belief to an escalator. You keep taking one step after another and there's always another one ready to place your foot on."

If you can believe in an escalator, why not try believing in the power of your own mind? Your mind can uproot any false belief and plant another one that you choose to cultivate. Belief is a *Choice*!

I choose to create a belief system that works for me!

At this point during Boot Camp, I ask the participants to give me one thing they believe without a shadow of a doubt. Here are some of the things they've said:

"I believe that I am on the right path."
"I believe in love."
"I believe there is a God."
"I believe my belief creates my experience."
"I believe that I will survive at all costs."
"I believe that I have to do things to make people like me."
"I believe it's never too late to start over."
"I believe that people are basically good."
"I believe that my cup is half full. But I want to believe that it is completely full. Forget the empty part altogether."
"I believe that I'm starting to believe."

What is your one belief?

Attention: When we pay attention to our behavior, we begin to notice patterns. These patterns are being created by our beliefs. Our core beliefs are those things that we have developed since birth. We go through stages of belief. First, we inherit the beliefs of our parents or influential adults in our lives. We then often abandon those beliefs to search for our own individual beliefs. As we mature, we develop beliefs based on experience. These beliefs are now embedded in our personality and life patterns develop based on what we have accepted as our belief system.

Our job, this week, will be to recognize our core beliefs and make a conscious decision as to whether or not they are servicing us. For instance, I used to believe that a hole in my heart prohibited me from playing sports. I was told this. I believed this. Until one day, I decided to take matters into my own hands. I went and joined the crew team at my college. I made varsity lightweight and never looked back.

Note: Years later, when I was dancing on Broadway as Riff in "West Side Story," I was asked to see a specialist to make sure I wasn't exacerbating the hole in my heart. **IT WAS GONE!** I still have a murmur, but I kind of like the extra beat so I'm okay with that.

"It is done unto you as you believe."
Matthew 9:29

Directives for the Week: On a regular daily basis, ask yourself, *"What do I believe?"* More importantly, make sure you know *WHY* you believe what you believe.

Continue with your morning journal. Only this week, as you wake up, ask yourself the following questions:

1. Name one thing I definitely believe.

2. Why do I believe it?

3. Do I wish to continue believing this thing?

4. If I don't wish to believe it, what can I replace it with?

Remember: You get to decide what you believe. If there are beliefs left over from "Your Story," and you don't have a need for them any more, dump them. It's time to make room for beliefs that will take you where you want to go.

I believe I can FLY...I believe I can touch the SKY!

WEEK FOUR

Day Two

Meditation: There is a Truth within, an Infinite Truth, which washes across the Universe with clarity and purpose.   A knowing so pure and intimate, it speaks beyond words into the deepest feeling of the soul.   There, in the face of such Truth you will find your Higher Self.

"Inner peace is beyond victory or defeat."
Bhagavad Gita

Communication: Spending a week analyzing your beliefs is an endeavor of a seeker of Truth.   As you question the reasons for these beliefs to even have a presence in your life, you are beginning to understand how your life has evolved.   More importantly, you are learning that your future is yours to create.   Building a foundation of beliefs that empower you to succeed is a goal that will be honored and achieved.   How does this make you feel?

- Make a list of the beliefs that have come up this week.

- What beliefs have you decided to embrace?

- If you are in a group, share your thoughts. Keep mindful of a time allotment.   No cross-talk.   Own up to beliefs that are hard to shake.

Remember: The first step to succeeding at anything is a willingness to do the work. If you find yourself frustrated by beliefs that you feel you can't shake, just tell yourself you are *willing* to shake them.   That intention alone will create a breakthrough.

Accountability: Make an inventory of the directives and how well you accomplished them.

    1. Did you write each morning?

    2. Did you pay ***ATTENTION*** to the beliefs as they arose?

    3. Did you conclude each day with an assessment of how you did?

If not, why not?

Don't allow excuses to give you a way out. Excuses are just another name for failure. If you want to find an excuse, you will. If you want to succeed, you won't have time for excuses.

Quotes from Boot Camp

"Is it even possible that I don't believe in myself? Unfortunately, I think it is."

"Belief and Faith and Religion all get mixed up for me. And I don't like talking about God. I need something real to believe in."

"Today, right here in this room, I believe that things can

be different from what they have been."

"I still don't know what I believe. But I am willing to figure it out. That's how it works, right?"

"I feel like I should have a garage sale given the number of beliefs I'm ready to throw away. But I don't really want anyone else to buy them either."

Continue with this week's directives!

Believe you can...and you will!

BELIEF

SPIRITUAL BOOT CAMP

BELIEF

WEEK FIVE

BE PRESENT

WEEK FIVE

Day One

Meditation: (Ten minute minimum)

Allow the following words to resonate with you in whatever way feels right. Use it as a suggestion, a springboard to whatever comes next. Empty your mind and feel it fill up with a vibrant, peaceful energy.

> *"You are never alone or helpless.*
> *The force that guides the stars guides you too."*
> *Shrii Shrii Anandamurti*

Communication: Last week, I asked you who you believed yourself to be. The reason for that is simple. Belief is tied to self-worth. There is a Spiritual worth to all of mankind. In that place of Truth, we are all perfect, complete expressions of God. However, when we base our self-worth on the relative facts and not the Absolute Truth, we quite often come up short. To make matters worse, we turn this acceptance of the facts into a belief.

It becomes an endless circle of believing what we see and creating more of the same, instead of believing the Truth and creating something better.

- Write out the list of beliefs from your weekly journal, continuing on from Day Two of last week. How do they stack up? Can you see where you life is headed based on your current beliefs?

- Now make a list of the beliefs you have decided to cultivate. Can you see how beliefs are tied to self-worth and to the manifestation of your desires?

- Using the blank pages provided at the end of this chapter, write out a description of who you believe yourself to be. If it feels dishonest, so what? All you need to know is that regardless of how it feels, it is the Truth! Read it out loud to yourself and hear it as the Truth.

- If you are in a group, read aloud your description of yourself. Discuss the way it makes you feel reading this out loud in front of people. Keep mindful of a time allotment. No cross-talk, but keep notes on what resonates with you.

<u>Descriptions from past Boot Campers</u>:

"I am capable, stable, financially secure and unstoppable!"

"I didn't always know my connection to GOD. And to be perfectly honest, I do forget myself sometimes. But it's always a nice surprise when I find myself again. Like, "Oh yeah, right. That's wasn't me. This is me."

"I am tall, dark and handsome…on a Spiritual plane."

"I am Compassion, Love, Responsibility, Self-awareness, Integrity, Faith and more than I could have ever imagined. The difference is, now I imagine!"

**Intention**: This week's Intention/Directive is to _**Be Present.**_

Now this might seem like an easy thing to do, _**Be Present.**_ But how many times have you been driving somewhere and suddenly realize that you don't remember getting where you are.   What was I thinking these past few minutes?   Where was I?   Well, you weren't really here. Your body was here but your mind was miles away.

Ever had someone talk to you and tune them out?   Ever gotten bored by something you were doing and, while you continued to do it, you left the building and thought about something, ANYTHING else?

Once while I was performing in **42nd Street** (as the tap dancing fool, Billy Lawlor), I was in front of an audience of twenty-eight hundred people, tapping away on top of a giant dime. I had been performing in the show for over a year and, by this point, I was on auto-pilot. I started thinking about where I was going to have dinner that night after the show. All of a sudden, the number was over, people were applauding and I couldn't remember which number I had just finished. I had to look down to see what I was wearing to figure out where I was. You'd have thought the dime would have given me a hint. Scary! That was _**NOT**_ being present.

> _"By watching the mechanics of the mind,_
> _you step out of its resistance patterns,_
> _and you can then allow the present moment to be."_
> _Eckhart Tolle_

The importance of being present cannot be overstated. Our culture is so committed to living in the future, we seldom even taste our food anymore.   Moments in time are passing us by and we're the poorer for it. We're trying so hard to "get somewhere" that we don't appreciate the beauty of where we are.

The other day, my daughter asked me to come outside and look at a flower she found. I was busy at the time doing something that I'm sure was of monumental importance. She smiled and ran back out to look at the flower. From the window, I could see her staring at this flower with such delight. I got up, put my work down and went out to join her. She was so excited to show me this flower that had only bloomed that morning. "It wasn't there yesterday and here it is today," she said in amazement. I will always remember that moment. And I might have missed it, if I hadn't decided to be present.

During one Boot Camp, I realized that being present forces us to live Intuitively. If we persist on living in the moment, we open the floodgates to a world of Divine energy. It is the most authentic of worlds when we bring our *Attention* to the present moment. There is a power unparalleled, waiting to be tapped and it's only found in the *Present*.

You cannot intuit God in the past or in the future.
Spirit is only found in the Present.

Attention: In order to live in the present, you must bring your *Attention* into every situation. You must be vigilant in focusing your mind and using the strength of your mental muscle to keep it focused.

Directives for the Week: Continue with your morning journal. Follow your thoughts and write them down. Don't allow your mind to drift, without following it. Stay present.

During the week, be aware of when you are present and when you are not. When you catch yourself drifting away, ask yourself what it is you are stepping away from. This can be very enlightening. Make notes on those times and circumstances when you "phone it in."

1. This week, you will take one hour a day to do something that fills you from within. Something that you enjoy. A break from your usual schedule. If you normally go for a jog in the morning, that doesn't count. Take a specific hour for yourself where you will **Be Present** for the entire time doing something you like doing.

Some Boot Camp outings: *Roller skating, hiking, a trip to the museum, a needlepoint class, going to the movies, pole dancing (really), shooting hoops, playing the piano...*

Remember: Only you know what makes you blissful, what fills you up. It's up to you to take the time to honor yourself by showing up. Don't let this week slide by without giving yourself the present of **Being Present.** You might miss the most wonderful flower, or a chance to see delight in the eyes of a child. You might miss a moment that is Truly "Amazing."

"We should erase the thoughts of yesterday that would rob us of today's happiness!"
Ernest Holmes

There's a reason they call it...THE PRESENT!

WEEK FIVE

Day Two

Meditation: (Ten minute minimum)

Repeat the following, allowing the final **I** to take you into the silence.

I AM HERE
I AM HERE
I AM
I AM
I
I

Communication: How does it feel ***Being Present*** in each moment? What things took you out of the moment and caused you to either look back or race forward?

- Reflect on the past few days (since your last day) and notate any shifts in attitude, feeling or perception. Are you happier, more energetic? Does the world seem larger?

I ask this question about the world seeming larger because, very often, when we practice the presence, we become aware of our connection to everything around us. The intimate details of a tree somehow seem to resonate on a deeper level. The sounds of the ocean become familiar, as if they are emanating from our very soul. I know this can all sound kind of "woo-woo," but there comes a time when the unexplainable shifts into the understandable. ***Being Present*** is a catalyst for such a shift. We might not have the exact words for what we perceive, but words can only take us so far. There is that within each of us that goes beyond the words, beyond the knowledge, beyond the feeling.

- If you are in a group, share your thoughts, your feelings, and your perceptions. Don't be worried about how they are being heard. Just stay present and allow yourself to explore. Keep mindful of your time allotment. No cross-talk.

Accountability:

1. Did you write each morning?

2. Did you take the hour each day for yourself?

3. Did you *make* notes of when and why you detached from the present?

If not, why not?

By now I would expect you to answer all questions in the positive. If, for whatever reason you answered in the negative, make a better effort. Remember: If you don't think you're worth the effort, who will?

Quotes from Boot Camp

"Spiritual Practice really brings up the GUNK. And being present, I can't pretend it isn't there."

"Authenticity can be scary! I think that's why sometimes I run away into the hinterlands of my mind."

"Sometimes it's all hurry up and make it happen. Make

WHAT happen? I don't even know anymore, I'm just hurrying up."

Continue with this week's directives!

I keep My Word and stay <u>AWAKE</u> in the moment!

BE PRESENT

_____

_____

_____

_____

_____

_____

_____

_____

_____

_____

_____

_____

_____

_____

_____

_____

_____

_____

_____

_____

_____

_____

_____

_____

_____

_____

_____

_____

_____

_____

_____

_____

_____

_____

_____

_____

_____

_____

_____

_____

_____

_____

_____

_____

_____

_____

_____

BE PRESENT

_____

_____

_____

_____

_____

_____

_____

_____

_____

_____

_____

_____

_____

_____

_____

_____

_____

_____

_____

_____

_____

_____

_____

SPIRITUAL BOOT CAMP

WEEK SIX

PATIENCE

WEEK SIX

Day One

Meditation: (Ten minute minimum)

As you prepare for today's meditation, consider the words of Dr. Ernest Holmes:

*"I stand in the midst of eternal opportunity,
which is forever presenting me with the evidence of its
full expression.
I am joy, peace and happiness.
I radiate Life, I am Life.
There is but one Life and that Life is my life now!"*

In the present moment, Life is pouring Itself through you on every level. Take this time to experience this Life affirming energy.

Communication: Many of us have not lived our lives fully present. We always found ways to escape into tomorrow or drift back into yesterday. Today was something that we needed to "get through." In the famous words of Scarlett O'Hara, "I'll think about it tomorrow." And then it was tomorrow, presenting itself with pretty much the same scenario. Only now, we're creating a "dread cycle" where we build up more fear and anxiety around something than it ever warranted.

Being present allows us to take things as they come and know the Truth about them, based on our knowledge that it is all Spirit. In a split precious moment, you are capable of turning your life around merely by becoming present, remembering who you are and co-creating your life with the Divine Energy that is always there to be tapped into.

In order for you to communicate this week's journey into the present, and in order for you to stay fully present as you sift through the past, try this exercise:

- Close your eyes and listen to the sounds of the room.
- Take a deep breath and breathe in the smells.
- Touch your fingertips gently to the sides of your face.
- Now move your hands away from your face and slowly open your eyes.

When you feel ready, on the blank pages provided at the end of this chapter, begin to journal your experience with this week's directive. How did it feel staying present? What does it feel like? How easy was it for you? What were the benefits? How often were you able to actively be present?

What was it like taking an HOUR a day to focus on being present in your Life, doing what YOU wanted to do?

As you begin to write, if you feel yourself drifting into your memories, go back to the top of the exercise. Close your eyes and listen to the sounds of the room. Continue through the steps until you are present again. Then go back to writing. Allow yourself to do this as often as you like throughout your journaling.

- If you are in a group, do this exercise together. Then begin sharing your week with the group. Keep mindful of a time allotment. No cross-talk, but feel free to continue the "present" exercise throughout the Communication part of Boot Camp.

Intention: This week's Intention/Directive is *Patience.*

"True Patience is Knowing!"

I have to admit that I have not always been a patient man. I was one of those people who never read the directions, because it took too long and I was certain that I could get it done faster if I just "did it." The truth is, I usually had to go back and read the directions anyway. So how does that link up to *Knowing?*

Knowing that Life is always working as planned, and that there is good in everything, takes the impatience out of living. I'm not in a hurry, because I like where I am. I'm not trying to "get" somewhere else. Consequently, I am always where it is best for me to be. I know this can sound like a lot of New Age stuff, crystals and incense, magnet rocks and such; and I'm not against any of it really. I just don't rely on them to make things happen – they're fun accoutrement. So, as I Believe that my life is Good, it is! As I stay in the Present, and know the truth about who and what I am, I AM. And there isn't any reason for me to be impatient given what I know. But I have to keep knowing it on a daily basis.

Impatience is a SHOULD...
Patience is an I AM.

Life is filled with "SHOULDS." I should do this today, but I'd rather do that. I should have done this yesterday but I didn't, I did that other thing. I REALLY should do this now but instead I think I'll do something else. I should change that about me. Why? Clearly, the problem here is that what you think you should do, you don't want to do. Ever try to make a child put on a sweater when they're not cold? I did. It didn't go well. You know why? SHE WASN'T COLD! I learned that lesson quickly as the father of twin two year olds. Children don't live in the world of "shoulds." They just are.

Patience comes when a person is present in his or her life and is in touch with their Divine Purpose. Patience isn't slowness. On the contrary, it is vibrant with energy and passion.   When I am patient I have the ability to accomplish anything and everything.

Patience is being connected to your True Self.

Attention: Pay attention this week to how you work with patience. Notice when you have patience and when you don't. There's a reason for both scenarios. Pay attention to what comes before a loss of patience and what follows. You'll be amazed at the effect impatience has on the body.

Now I'm certain that you can all find reasons why your impatience is manifesting. There's much to be impatient with. If you drive a car, work with children, are married, have in-laws, have parents, have neighbors, are alive... you will be able to find "reasons" to be impatient. Pay attention to these "reasons" this week.

Directives for the Week: Continue with your morning journal.

When you wake up, make a special note of how you are feeling. Sometimes, we wake up anxious. What's that about? Occasionally, we wake up tired. Other times we wake up, bolt out of bed and are ready to meet the day. I love those days. Write about it.

Specifically, take time this week to focus your *Attention* on being patient. Notice when you are making an effort to be patient and when it just happens naturally. Catch yourself in the act. Make a mental note - same goes for when you "lose it."

1. At the end of the day, write out your "Mental Notes to Yourself" and expand on the event by asking yourself, "Why did I react that way?"

2. That's all for this week other than to say BE DILIGENT! Notice yourself...and you will KNOW YOURSELF.

Patience Creates the Perfect Flow.

WEEK SIX

Day Two

Meditation: Relax - Release - Allow

I come to the silence to hear.
I listen for the thoughts without words.
A feeling creeps into my awareness.
You are there in the feeling.
I smile, I laugh, I cry, I know.

Communication: In the past few days, how has patience been working for you? Do you find yourself to be a patient person? Are you as patient on the inside as you are perceived to be on the outside? Are you becoming aware of the "buttons" you possess? What are they? What makes you impatient?

In one of the Boot Camps, it was shared that patience came easy to this particular gentleman. However, upon reflection, he realized that his patience was the result of apathy. He'd been disappointed so often, and with such disturbing results, that he'd stopped trying. He'd given up on many of his dreams and was settling for just "getting by." But to those who met him he was perceived as a patient man.

I found his sharing very perceptive. He didn't like the patience week because he wanted to get rid of his patience and go out there and knock down walls. What he realized was that he wanted to get rid of his apathy and step back into his personal "Circle of Energy."

- What's your story surrounding patience? How

have the last few days differed for you in relation to your level of patience and impatience? Write it in your journal and expand on it with each new day and awareness.

- What sort of things are you feeling when you wake up in the morning? How do you perceive yourself?

- For group work, share your personal story. Are you patient? Are you sure? When are you impatient? Why? Keep mindful of a time allotment. No cross-talk.

Remember: There is no correct answer to any of these questions. There are only YOUR answers and they are meant to inform you, not depress you. Don't allow yourself to second-guess yourself. The journey is perfect.

Accountability:

1. Did you write each morning?

2. Are you paying attention to yourself in terms of patience?

3. Have you written down your feelings first thing in the morning?

If not, why not?

Quotes from Boot Camp

"I just feel like people should know better! How can you be patient with these people?"

"I'm always running late and so I'm always frustrated. Hard to be patient when you're always late."

"Patience has to have a line, you know, a line between being patient and BLOWING UP."

"I've noticed that impatience spreads pretty quickly."

"For me, patience isn't waiting. It's living in the moment. It's actually something tangible, for me."

Continue with this week's directives!

Perfect Timing is a Choice!

PATENCE

_____

_____

_____

_____

_____

_____

_____

_____

_____

_____

_____

_____

_____

_____

_____

_____

_____

_____

_____

_____

_____

_____

_____

_____

PATIENCE

WEEK SEVEN

LISTEN/RESOLVE

WEEK SEVEN

Day One

Meditation: (Ten minute minimum)

*"It isn't until you come to a Spiritual understanding of
who you are,
not necessarily a religious feeling, but deep down, the
Spirit within,
that you can begin to take control of your life."*
Oprah Winfrey

For the next ten or so minutes, take control of your mind. Bring the concept of *Patience* into your meditation. Keep it simple, peaceful and loving. Be gentle with your thoughts, guiding them back to *Patience.*

Communication: Spending a week, mindful of the level of patience in my life, has always led me to certain facts that I might not have discovered otherwise. For instance, it never occurred to me that I didn't have to have the answer to every question as it was posed in any given moment. Not having the answer did not mean that I was ill-prepared or stupid. Perhaps, I discovered, living the question for a while was the very answer I needed. I go back to my mantra, "I know nothing, now what can I learn?" It really opens up the floodgates of potentiality.

As you made your way through the week, did you notice how many times you were challenged with situations that called on you to exhibit patience? One morning, one of our Boot Campers said that every week, when the Intention was announced, he felt like it was a "calling all cars" for whatever directive that was given. Patience week meant that every opportunity for patience was on its way. Watch out!

*"I was on the freeway, the 405, and I found myself stuck between these two trucks. Me, in my little MG Midget, boxed in on the freeway at rush hour. And then I remembered it was '**Patience Week**' and I thought, of course."*

What's gone on in your life this week? How many opportunities did you have to be patient? Were you able to succeed? If not, did you look behind the impatience and see what was causing it? Overall, how did it go?

- Take a look at your notes from the week. Rate your days on a one to ten scale for your ability to exhibit patience.

On the blank pages provided at the end of this chapter, put a line of dots indicating where your patience level would have landed on a one to ten rating scale. For example:

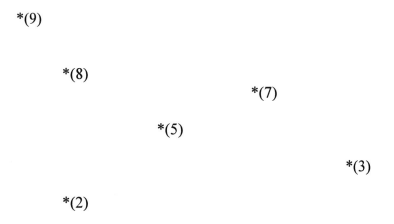

*(9)

        *(8)

                        *(7)

              *(5)

                              *(3)

        *(2)

Now connect the dots with a line. How crazy a roller coaster is your "patience" level?

The object here is to create a balanced life. To the degree that you have control over your mind, your thoughts, your beliefs; to that degree will you have control over your life. Patience, like everything else, is a choice! We are always at choice. We just aren't always patient. Just look at the line you drew and you'll see the ride you're on.

- If you are in a group, do this exercise together. Discuss the "ride" you're taking and how much control you have over it. Keep mindful of a time allotment. No cross-talk. Be patient with one another.

Intention: This week's Intention/Directive is ***Listen/ Resolve.***

"I listen for the sound of my Authentic Voice!"

Two parts to this week's Intention.

Part One: *Listen*

The world is a very loud place - lots to hear and many voices crowding the airwaves. Everywhere we turn, we are assaulted by *noise*. The art of listening has become quite uncommon. Most often, in the midst of a conversation, I can actually see the person I'm speaking to not listening to what I'm saying in anticipation of what he or she plans to say. I certainly catch myself in that trap as well. People today speak over one another as though it were the only way to converse. Our contemporary playwrights are genius at capturing the way we talk without listening, interrupt without apology and communicate without thinking. We recognize it and laugh our heads off because it's so true.

Listening to what's outside our mind is one thing, but listening to what's going on inside our mind and beyond, now that's another thing altogether. I believe that as we become more attuned to our Authentic Voice, our God Self, we will be able to navigate the 'surround sound,' that is the world we live in, without becoming susceptible to its sometimes exhausting energy.

"I hear based on where I'm at."

We all do. We hear what we want to hear, based on what we need to hear. Often, we hear based on our fears and our doubts. But are we listening, keeping our minds open and our thoughts free from experience? Are we able to listen as a child for the "new" thought, the new awareness, the new Truth? Are we able to distinguish the authentic from the plastic? I believe we can! If we "hear based on where we're at," then we need to inform ourselves that we are in *Heaven*, and we are ready to hear the angels sing. Why not? After all, "It is done unto us as we believe."

Part Two: *Resolve everything in the moment*

One of the reasons we have such a hard time listening for the "new" is because we're so clogged up with the "old." Every time we procrastinate and put something off until tomorrow, we're taking up precious space in our mind with something that we have labeled *TO DO.* These things become like little sinkers on the end of a fishing pole. Put too many on the rod and eventually it snaps. You won't be catchin' anything in that ocean.

Why resolve everything in the moment? Because you can

- because you have the ability - and because you have the choice. A very funny writer in our Boot Camp stated one morning that her mother was like "General Patton." "My whole childhood was regimented. We did everything we were told and completed it like we were vying for medals. I think one year she actually did give out medals." She shared later that she realizes now that she stopped doing certain things as a reaction to her mother. Procrastination was her way of getting back at someone who wasn't even alive anymore.

Leaving things unresolved is like having a backed-up sink and not taking care of it. Eventually, you have to unclog it. The longer you wait, the more disgusting the contents. If you deal with each item as it goes down the drain, it goes down a lot easier.

Attention: Pay attention this week to what you are hearing. Listen to the sounds of the world around you. Listen at home, at the office, in the market, at the bank. Listen to what the world is saying. Listen also for your reaction to what you are hearing. Listen within.

In your daily meditation, shut off the noise, the sounds, and the chatter of your own thoughts. Listen intently for the Authentic Self. It could be a thought. It could be a feeling. It could be a color. Whatever it is, _allow_ yourself to experience it. Enter the silence, listen, and see what comes next.

Directives for the Week: Continue with your morning journal.

1. *Listen/Hear/Allow*—Meditate each morning following your morning journaling for a minimum of ten minutes. Your only objective is to *Listen.*

2. Resolve everything in the moment. Do not allow anything to go unresolved, no matter how insignificant it may appear. Make an immediate response to everything that comes up.

Do it NOW!

WEEK SEVEN

Day Two

Meditation: *Listen*

> *I have discovered a secret place within,*
> *where the thought goes into a mountain high above the*
> *din of the world.*
> *I have found in this mountain a place of peace and rest,*
> *A place of joy and comfort to the heart.*
> *I have found that the Secret Place of God is within my*
> *own Soul.*
> *I will listen for Thy Voice.*

Communication: What do you hear when you listen? Are you able to enter the quiet and hear? How is the world around you responding to you, now that you are listening to it?

Are you able to respond to each situation with a resolute attitude? Often, when we allow things to go unresolved it's because we somehow think we can't or don't have the capacity to resolve them. Sometimes we just won't, because we resent General Patton.

- Use this opportunity to write your thoughts about this week thus far. As you write, listen to what you are thinking.

- For group work, share your personal story and keep notes on what you hear yourself thinking. Keep mindful of your time allotment. No cross-talk.

Accountability:

1. Did you write each morning?

2. Have you kept up with your meditation in the morning?

3. Are you resolving things in the moment?

I'm just going to know that you are doing it ALL.

Quotes from Boot Camp

"Love rights the space,
I exist long into the void.
And out of the darkness a constant battery –
My own assault. A Waging war that never ends.
And I cry to be held, the answers to be given.
Tell me the truth, it SCREAMS – Tell me the Truth.
A breath - The truth - a soft whisper, the faint beat of my heart.
The breathing slows and from the silence,
A whisper pierces and resonates,
As a bolt of lightning against the black sky
....SSHHH.....I am Here. LISTEN."

Written by: Rob Arbogast
(Boot Camp, Fall '07)

Continue with this week's directives!

"SSHHH…I am Here. LISTEN!"

LISTEN/RESOLVE

SPIRITUAL BOOT CAMP

LISTEN/RESOLVE

WEEK EIGHT

BOUNDARIES/PRIORITIES

WEEK EIGHT

Day One

Meditation: (Ten minute minimum)

> *"I do because I can. I can because I know.*
> *I know because I Am."*

As you continue to listen from within your meditation, allow your mind to know the Truth, that you can accomplish whatever you decide to accomplish. Hear what comes up and resolve it in the moment. You can, because you know you can. You know because YOU ARE the I AM!

Communication:

"When I listen my whole world calms down."

"I am bigger than anything I encounter. That's fun to know."

"The world is a very loud place when you actually stop and listen to it. I need to stop more often, I think."

"Most of the noise I hear seems to be coming from my own head."

"I feel like there's a committee in my head. They all talk at the same time. Nobody's listening."

One thing I recognize about my life is that I have become desensitized to the sounds around me. I walk by a Starbucks and see people with their iPods, working on their computers and I realize that we are all trying to create a space of our own in the midst of a very busy world. It's interesting that we now create space for ourselves on the Web, My Space, Your Space, Our Space...it's ALL SPACE really! But what can we make of it? That's the question.

What we need to listen to most is what we are saying to ourselves. How are we reacting to what we are hearing? What do we tell ourselves? Do we even take the time to hear what we think, or do we live reactionary lives that fly by at an alarming pace? It's a choice that we can resolve in this present moment. This past week has been designed to prove to you that you can resolve anything in the present moment.

"The chatter in my head is the lack of decision. Decisions quiet my mind."

Resolving things in the moment frees up the next moment to the unexpected possibility of the new. This is what we are looking for, an opening to a higher conscious awareness. Listening to the silence, resolving in the moment, hearing the Authentic Self; all of this begins the journey to that opening.

- Make a list of what you learned about yourself this week. Were you able to resolve things in the moment? Did you experience a new communication level as you listened more clearly?

- As you write, listen to what you are thinking. See if you can combine listening with expressing your thoughts. Ultimately that is our goal: to connect to the Source in such a way as to allow it to inform us on every level.

- If you are in a group, share your experience with one another. Try to listen as others speak, without judgment or opinion. See what happens. Share it. Keep mindful of a time allotment. No cross-talk.

Intention: This week's Intention/Directive is **Boundaries/ Priorities.**

"I feel like I've been in a dream and I'm just waking up!"

Part One: **Boundaries**

There are many types of boundaries. Much like the witches in Oz, there are good boundaries and there are bad boundaries. The good ones are those that you set for specific, constructive reasons. The bad ones are those that go up as defense mechanisms for perceived "evil" and ones that were created by past experiences that we might not even be aware of. We call those "walls" and we spend much of our lives climbing over them or hitting them to the point of exhaustion.

Our purpose this week is to identify our boundaries and tag them as either useful or damaging. Once we do that, we can then go about the business of obliterating the walls and opening the horizons to a brighter day. We might even get to meet the Wizard, and eventually realize that we had the answer all along.

"Self-image sets the boundaries of individual accomplishment."
Maxwell Maltz

Part Two: **Priorities**

How do you decide what to do? What makes one thing important to accomplish and another thing put aside for later? Why do you do the things you do? It's important to know.

There are two reasons for doing things - obligation and passion. Occasionally, we do things because we have nothing else to do, and that falls in line with not really doing, but existing. We're talking here about things you "decide" to do.

Are you doing them because you feel you "have to?" Or are you doing them because you are passionate about the doing? Mother Theresa once said that fulfilling one's purpose in life is to find one's passion and live it. Are you doing that?

Attention: Pay attention this week to the boundaries that exist in your life. See where you have created them for a reason and where they seem to have appeared out of nowhere. Does this boundary meet your needs or is it keeping you from them? Is it a good boundary or a bad boundary?

Put your attention on what you are doing, where your priorities resonate and where they don't.

Directives for the Week: Continue with your morning journal.

1. Each morning when you wake up, make a list of your priorities for the day. Jot down how they make you feel.

2. Before you go to sleep each night, go over your list of priorities from the morning. Did you succeed at meeting them, or did they get pushed aside for other, more immediate priorities? Note how this played out in your day.

3. Keep an ongoing list of boundaries as you continue through the week. Next to each one write either GOOD or BAD. You can also write down PENDING if you aren't sure.

Boundaries and priorities are directly linked to your self-worth. When we love ourselves, respect ourselves and insist on only that which will feed our souls and nourish our minds, we prioritize and set boundaries that reflect a healthy understanding of who we are.

"There is Good for me and I ought to have it!"
Emma Curtis Hopkins

WEEK EIGHT

Day Two

Meditation: ***Boundaries/Priorities***

My mind stays open to a field of infinite possibility.
Air is plenty, sky is limitless, light is ever present.
I see, I feel, I smell, I touch, and yet I never move.
I AM movement. I AM sky. I AM touch.
My walls have no purpose.
My boundaries have no reason.
The only thing to do...is TO BE!

Communication: I've heard it said that boundaries are signposts of how far we are willing to go in any situation. It is also how far we are willing to let someone in. Is it safe to be an open door for anyone to enter? How open are you to hearing what others have to say? How well do you take criticism? Are you conscious of other people's boundaries?

Where are your walls? Are you closed in by your own inability to go beyond your comfort zone? What is your comfort zone? Is it something that feeds you, or holds you back? How comfortable do you need to be? Where's the line? Where's the boundary?

Are you your number one priority? When you made your list of priorities for the day, were you on that list? What position were you in?

- As you ponder the answers to the above questions, notice how you feel. On the blank pages provided at the end of this chapter, write down your feelings.

- Also, on the blank pages, make a list of your current priorities and number them in terms of importance. When you are done, see if the amount of time you focus on each of these priorities matches up with their placement of importance.

- For group work, share your personal story. Do the exercise regarding the priorities and read them to the group, commenting on how they match up with your level of attention to each priority. Keep mindful of a time allotment. No cross-talk.

Accountability:

1. Did you write each morning and evening?

2. Have you kept up with your meditation in the morning?

3. Did you make a list of your priorities and label them either good or bad or pending?

"There is good in the world and I ought to have it!"
Emma Curtis Hopkins

To have it…you have to take it!

Quotes from Boot Camp

"This week I saw for the first time that I wasn't my number one priority. I put everyone else before me."

"I don't trust myself to choose wisely, so the walls go up."

"This thing called, 'other people,' forces my hand to create boundaries."

"Talk about crossing boundaries, my mother ought to have a company called www.MATCH.MOM. She thinks it's okay to fix me up with whomever she wants. I need to set that boundary and I'll call it GOOD!"

"My priorities aren't the same from day to day, especially now."

Continue with this week's directives!

We can do it all! The question is, in what order?

BOUNDARIES/PRIORITIES

_____

_____

_____

_____

_____

_____

_____

_____

_____

_____

_____

_____

_____

_____

_____

_____

_____

_____

_____

_____

_____

_____

_____

_____

BOUNDARIES/PRIORITIES

WEEK NINE

LIFE FORCE

WEEK NINE

Day One

THE HALF WAY POINT

Congratulations, you have made it to the halfway point of Spiritual Boot Camp. If you've stuck to the program, you are much more aware of what is going on inside your mind and you should be seeing changes reflected in the way your life is unfolding. They say knowledge is power – well, Self-knowledge is Self-power.

Now, it's time to recommit to the program and, by doing so, recommit to *Yourself*. Begin your meditation today with the following:

Meditation: (Ten minute minimum)

I rise to a higher consciousness. I step into my Divine Power!

Repeat this at least three times. Allow yourself to hear the words as they are formed in your mouth. Listen as your "Voice" repeats the Truth of who and what you are capable of being and doing. You can, and do, "rise" above every situation into a higher consciousness of Truth. You ARE Divine Power.

Communication: Following your meditation, take a moment to think about *YOUR WORD*. How does it feel, eight weeks later? Is it applicable to what you've learned about yourself? In terms of priorities, has Your Word become an important part of your day-to-day life? Are **You** your number one priority?

"Action expresses priorities."
Mahatma Gandhi

Talk is cheap and it's getting cheaper by the year. It's all too easy to say what you are going to do. Everyone has a plan, a dream, a tomorrow they will tell you about. But until they can show you, it's all just feathers in the wind. If you have a priority, and really make it important, you will back it up with *Action*.

I once heard an acting teacher say to someone, "If you were arrested for being an actor, would there be enough evidence to convict you? Or would you get off because they could only pin you with being a waiter?" Point made, at least it was to that guy. Without naming names, he's a very successful movie actor today.

- Look at your lists from throughout the week. What are they telling you about your commitment level to your proclaimed priorities? What do you need to know here? Does something need to change? Write out a new priority list addressing these insights.

- How would you feel if you were to drop all of your boundaries - good, bad and pending? Would you feel vulnerable or excited for the future? Spend some time with this option. View it from many sides and see if it feels like something to step into.

- If you are in a group, share your feelings on these topics. Keep mindful of a time allotment. No cross-talk.

Intention: This week's Intention/Directive is *Life Force.*

"Kid, I've flown from one side of this galaxy to the other,
and I've seen a lot of strange stuff,
but I've never seen 'anything' to make me believe
that there's one all-powerful Force controlling
everything."
Han Solo to Luke Skywalker

Revisiting **Star Wars**, with my eight-year-old son, has been an awesome experience. When I saw the movies the first time, I wasn't so in tune with metaphysics and New Thought. Now, watching the movie, I am blown away by how much Truth there is in the story. And I love that they use Han Solo to play the role of the reluctant hero. He wants proof, and the movie uses that opportunity to show him the proof.

There is a Life Force back of everything. It's not a separate entity predetermining our destiny, but an energy that moves through us and is there for us to use. It intuits through our mind and allows us to create based on our thoughts.

"Change your thinking, change your life."
Ernest Holmes

Depending on what thoughts we put into our mind, how we believe and what we believe, our world manifests proportionately. If I think (believe) success, I am successful. If I think (believe) love, I will experience love. If, conversely, I think (believe) lack - well, I just don't. I know how that movie ends. And thus our Life Force, flowing through us, *allows* us to be the co-creator of our own creations. Sometimes we're riding high and other times we're hitting bottom. It's an eternal roller coaster and yet it doesn't have to be. It's the same Life Force, whether we use it to create happiness or despair.

"I feel like there's a Life Force vampire roaming around and every now and then I'm pulled into its den and the life is sucked out of me."
Boot Camper

If we are aware enough to notice, we will always know which things create a flow of Life Force and which ones suck it out of us. For example: judgment, fear, stress, arguments, they all deplete the Life Force flow. Notice I said 'flow.' Your Life Force can never be depleted. You can put a kink in the hose and stop the flow, but you can never erase the Source.

Attention: Pay attention this week to what makes your heart sing and what gets stuck in your throat. Notice what fills you up and what leaves you empty. ***Allow*** yourself to be brutally honest with respect to what really does bring you happiness and what doesn't.

Directives for the Week: Continue with your morning journal.

1. Make a list of the areas in your life where you are being fed and nourished. Then write down those things that take away your Life Force. Do this impersonally and with respect for your past choices. Do this daily, refining the list as the week progresses.

2. Do one thing each day that activates your Life Force. Try to find new and different things that will accomplish this task.

LIFE FORCE

"May the Force be with you!"
Obi-Wan Kenobi

WEEK NINE

Day Two

Meditation: Today, as you meditate, *allow* your mind to "feel" the flow of energy in your body. Feel and hear the pulse and rhythm of your blood as it travels in perfect time through your body. Feel yourself living inside your skin. Feel the chair you are sitting in, or the air around you if you are standing. Become one with everything around you and then begin to feel the Universal Life Force that supports and holds you in its rhythm and song.

"Music and rhythm find their way into the secret places of the soul."
Plato

Communication: It is very clear to me that, when I take action in my life, when I make a strong decision to do something active, my Life Force starts to swell. As I move, so does the energy that is my soul. Passion is one way to measure Life Force. If you are passionate about what you are doing, you will always be increasing your Life Force. And you can feel when that happens.

I remember when I was opening in a new musical in Philadelphia. As the title character, I was to open the show by coming onstage alone and singing the first notes of the play acapella (without accompaniment). The note was given to me as I approached the stage and I was required to hold onto it until my cue to enter. Well, it was opening night and for some reason, once I got in place, we had to hold for ten minutes.

Somewhere around minute seven, I lost the note. I could

feel the energy in my body start to swell. Of course, this was fear, combined with excitement and uncertainty of the outcome. Just as I was about to go off and get the note, the cue light went on and I was caught. I walked onstage with my little lantern (I was playing a young Irish coal miner) and I began to sing. I looked out into the audience and realized how incredibly happy I was to be doing what I was doing. I completely forgot about the note, or whether or not I was in the right key. My Life Force came from behind and drove me right from that starting moment clear through to curtain call. Passion prevails! (I was about one half step above the note and I slipped down once the orchestra came in. No one noticed, or so they said.)

- In the past few days, have you noticed when you are energized and when you feel low? More importantly, have you made special note of what it is that causes you to feel one way or the other?

- When you actively decide to do something to increase your Life Force, what happens?

- For group work, share your personal story with one another. Pay close attention to the Life Force in the room. What causes it to shift? What propels you and what causes you to tune out? Keep mindful of a time allotment. No cross-talk.

Accountability:

1. Did you write each morning and evening, going over your discoveries and refining them as you go along?

2. Have you kept up with your meditation in the morning?

3. Have you made time to do something each day that activates your Life Force?

If not, make sure you know the reason you didn't do the work.

Quotes from Boot Camp

"Never force the Force!"

"Micromanaging every little thing about my life is exhausting. And it eats into my Life Force."

"I feel like I'm having spiritual contractions giving birth to this Life Force."

Continue with this week's directives!

Your purpose is your passion. Don't go looking for it. It will find you!

LIFE FORCE

WEEK TEN

PERFECTIONISM

WEEK TEN

Day One

Meditation: (Ten minute minimum)

> *"I am alive with energy. My Being sings with enthusiasm!"*

Take these words into your meditation. Regardless of the facts, no matter how you are feeling, speak these words knowing that there is a part of you, untouched, unmoved, never reactive, always flowing. It is your True Life Force. Activate It with your silence. Listen for It. Feel It. *Allow* It to inform you as you step into your own Energy Circle.

Communication: Do you like yourself? Do you respect your time? Do you allow others to take over your thoughts, ideas, and resources? Where do you fall in your list of priorities? Are you stuck with an image of someone who focuses on himself, or herself, as being too egocentric? What are you worth, exactly?

All priorities come from your assessment of who you are. A person who recognizes their true worth will always make decisions based on what is the best thing to do in any given moment. Priorities are easy to place for the man or woman who is resolute in their identity. Confidence comes from knowing who you are. It doesn't come from knowing what you are meant to do, your net worth, where you came from, or if you have any talent. None of these things has anything to do with who you are. Who you are informs those things. So who are you?

You are the presence of Spirit working, flowing through

you, creating a unique, individual personality of your choosing. You get to create whatever you want out of your life. Priorities are just things to enjoy making. They shouldn't be considered a "task" in order to get things done. They should be effortless based on the flow of Divine Energy, *your energy*.

From this place of True Identity, we can lower the walls and eliminate all boundaries, even good ones. We won't need them when we are centered in Truth. Things that once needed clear boundaries to keep them in place will now flow perfectly, for that is how they were meant to flow. I know myself and, therefore, the Universe knows me as I know me. I create only that which supports my highest consciousness. How great is that!

- Review your priority lists from this past week. Can you see how every one of your priorities can be traced back to who you are? Write a short paragraph on what this means to you. Keep it honest and concise.

- Did you resolve things in the moment? How did that feel?

- If you are in a group, share your paragraph with the others. How did your week go? Keep mindful of a time allotment. No cross-talk.

Intention: This week's Intention/Directive is ***Perfectionism.***

"They say that nobody is perfect.
Then they tell you practice makes perfect.
I wish they'd make up their minds."
Wilt Chamberlain

I love this quote. We live in a world that can be very confusing at times, if we let it. I grew up being told to continually work on becoming perfect at something. It didn't matter what it was, just find something you're good at and perfect it. So I tried playing the guitar. I was good, not perfect. I played the piano. I was okay, not even good. I sang. I could see perfection at times, but at others, I would miss the mark. Broadway, Hollywood, London, musicals, movies, record deals, all opportunities to show that I was Number One. Each one was a lesson in missing the mark. So close, so often and, by others standards, succeeding so brilliantly. But perfect? No! And it was never good enough for me.

It seems that the more you try to be perfect, the more you realize that it is an impossibility. For one thing, life is subjective. A perfect ten to one man could be a seven to another and then someone else comes along and calls it a three. So how do you even gauge what perfection is? It could drive you crazy spending a lifetime of trying to become perfect. And that's the problem. We are trying to **become** perfect when we already **are** perfect. How can you become what you already are? Good question!

"When you aim for perfection, you discover it's a moving target."
George Fisher

When Wilt Chamberlain writes, "I wish they'd make up their minds," it seems to me that he swishes it right through the net. (By the way, I was one of his 'ball boys' when he was playing basketball for the 76'ers in Philadelphia). We have to make up our minds that we already are perfect before we can actually tap into that perfection. We will never find it "out there." We do things from a place of perfection, not gain perfection from doing something well.

In changing your perspective about **perfection**, you will begin to step into an awareness of your True Potential far beyond anything you have experienced thus far. Instead of "reaching" for things, you will **allow** them to come to you.

*Perfection! It's an **inside job**.*

Attention: This week, pay attention to instances when you are **trying** to be perfect. Recognize your frustration when things aren't going the way you think they should be going. Put your attention on your inner Truth about perfection. See everything in a new light.

Directives for the Week: Continue with your morning journal. (Empty your mind of whatever thoughts you wish to release.)

1. Upon waking, take a moment after your morning journaling to meditate on the **perfection** that is the coming day. "Expect" only the good to be presented, recognizing that the perfection in you attracts the perfection of the world around you.

2. At night, write about your day. Be creative.

Perfection begins and ends with the Truth!

*You are already **PERFECT**!*

WEEK TEN

Day Two

Meditation: **God's world is perfect!**

*"Our mental attitude must be one of denial
toward every false condition that opposes the principle
of Life as one of absolute perfection."*
Ernest Holmes

Bring into meditation the following affirmation:

God's world is perfect, therefore my world is perfect!

Communication: During one Boot Camp session, someone shared that they could find the perfection in themselves, when they got quiet and the world was quiet around them. The problem started when they came out of meditation and had to deal with "other people" who clearly weren't perfect. Ever have that feeling?

I reminded myself, in that moment, that it was never about "other people," but always about me. My job is to see the perfection in others as easily I can see it in myself. If I'm seeing imperfection, I must be relating to something in myself that recognizes it. Now this isn't to say that I walk around like a lemming, following blindly the idea that there is only perfection in the world. I know that's not true on a human level. But I also know that what comes into my orbit is something for me to find the "good" in, for it is something for me to "know." Then someone else stated that she could always find the perfection in "others" but could never find it in herself.   She talked about spending her whole life trying to be perfect only to weigh in at "barely acceptable."

Again, trying to be perfect is a hopeless crusade.

- How often in the past few days did you find yourself striving for perfection? Do others, who seem to miss the mark, frustrate you? How does that affect you and your quest for inner peace?

- Can you find glimpses of your perfection in your meditation? Are you able to stay there and activate that energy into your daily living?

- For group work, share your thoughts with one another. Keep mindful of a time allotment. No cross-talk.

Accountability:

1. Did you start each day with the expectation of perfection?

2. Did you write about your day each night?

3. Are you paying attention to moments of perfectionism creeping into your Life Force?

If you are doing the work, you'll recognize the benefits.

Quotes from Boot Camp

"Trying to be perfect leads to paralysis."

"I already am perfect? Joke's on me then."

PERFECTIONISM

"I guess once I realize I already am perfect, it'll give a whole new meaning to perfectionism."

"So if I'm already perfect, why do I work so hard to prove it?"

Continue with this week's directives!

Don't look outside to prove your perfection!

PERFECTIONISM

PERFECTIONISM

_____

_____

_____

_____

_____

_____

_____

_____

_____

_____

_____

_____

_____

_____

_____

_____

_____

_____

_____

_____

_____

_____

_____

_____

_____

WEEK ELEVEN

INTENTION

WEEK ELEVEN

Day One

Meditation: (Ten minute minimum)

"Perfect God, Perfect Man, Perfect Being!"

Allow these words to percolate in your mind as you drift into the silence.

"Perfect God, Perfect Man, Perfect Being!"

Perfect God, the One Power of Love in the Universe, expressing through each of us perfectly, creating a Unity of Life accessible to all.

Drop everything else from your mind and focus on only this...

"Perfect God, Perfect Man, Perfect Being!"

Communication: By this point in the program, you have been asking yourself a lot of questions. You have purposefully been giving specific attention to things about yourself that are personal and revealing. Some of these things are merely facts that can be changed in the presence of a new belief, a better decision. Others are Truths that are irrefutable.

The Spiritual Truth that perfection lies within, and that we are that perfection to the degree that we **accept** this Truth, is a motivating force behind Spiritual "enlightenment." When you know this about yourself, there is no limit to what you can accomplish.

"Know thyself!"
Socrates

In today's world, we know ourselves based on so many things, most of which are transient. Who I was yesterday may be completely obliterated by what I know today and how I react given certain facts that are revealed to me. All of it shifts and all of it changes. The One changeless Truth in all of this is God. *"Perfect God, Perfect Man, Perfect Being!"* However, the **being** part of that equation is meant to be seen as a verb, not a noun - being perfect man, representing perfect God. It's the active part of Life.

How are you living this Truth? How does it show up in your life? What does it look like? How is it working for you?

- How did your week change with the expectation that it was guided by the perfection of the Universe? Did knowing that you already are perfect change your reactions to things throughout your day?

- Did you find that, at the end of your day, you were able to notice the shift in perception? How well did you do holding back from human perfectionism both with yourself and with others? Look back over what you wrote. Do you get it now?

*You already **ARE** perfect!*

- If you are in a group, share your thoughts. How does the consciousness of the room shift with each share? Does it move you from your own Truth or solidify it perfectly? Keep mindful of a time allotment. No cross-talk.

Intention: This week's Intention/Directive is **_Intention._**

"Our intention creates our reality."
Wayne Dyer

So, now that you know that you come from perfection, what are you going to do about it? Knowing something doesn't mean that you are living from that point of view. We have spent the past ten weeks focusing on Intentions. They have been specific to the week but, nonetheless, they have been directed toward an end result. That end result is an awareness of the Self, the higher Self.

The word "intention" means to act with purpose, to have a definite goal or destination in mind. It is the larger decision to create something in our lives. An intention to do, or to be or to have, sets the gears in motion for it to become a reality.

An intention is not a plan! It is what's behind the plan. Is it your intention to succeed? Is it your intention to struggle? Is it your intention to **allow** things to just happen? Intention is a first cousin to expectancy and yet it has its own set of distinctions. I remember once sitting in class with my teacher, Dr. David J. Walker, and hearing him say, "you know you have an intention if you actually DO IT! I can say I'm going to the movies but unless I look up the schedule, get in the car, drive to the theatre, buy the ticket (and popcorn) and climb into my seat, I can't really say I intended to go to the movies. If I don't do it I never intended it. I just **thought** about doing it.

*"Intentions are **thoughts activated!***

-163-

So, intentions are thoughts activated. Perhaps, given the previous scenario, I could have started out for the movies, noticed a breathtaking sunset on the horizon and ended up at the beach. Did I intend to go to the movies? Yes! It was just that a better intention came into play and then I followed through with that intention. Anything wrong with that? Depends on the movie, the sunset and the individual involved. If you were meeting someone at the movie you might have thought twice about shifting gears. Still and all, both intentions were put into play. They were both **activated.**

I bring up this last scenario because it came up in one of our Boot Camps. If intentions are thoughts activated, and we shift gears, did we ever have the first intention strongly enough to follow through with it? My answer to that is, don't drive yourself crazy. I believe that if I act on my intentions and stay open to the Life Force within, knowing that I fully expect my life to play out for my highest Good, then I will always know what to do, when to do it and who to do it with.

> *"Unless you marry intention to action,*
> *you end up with only a brief affair."*

Attention: Pay attention this week to your declared intentions. Are you acting on them, or are they just thoughts? Get clear on the difference between the two.

Directives for the Week: Continue with your morning journal.

1. Upon waking, make a list of your intentions for the day. Make sure not to make a list of your plans for the day, but your **intentions**. Remember: *Intentions are **thoughts activated**!*

2. This week choose an intention from your list and focus on the accomplishment of that intention. Follow through and see it to its fruition. Pick something uplifting, something that will feed your Life Force.

Don't just flirt with intention, make one and then act on it. Without the action it's nothing more than wishful thinking.

My intentions always manifest.
They climb every hill, ascend every peak.
I back my intention with my Word!

*Keep mindful of your **WORD**!*

WEEK ELEVEN

Day Two

Meditation: (Ten minute minimum)

"A good intention clothes itself with power."
Ralph Waldo Emerson

Sometimes the strongest action we can take is to step into the quiet of our own mind. There, we will find not only the answers but the questions that activate our Beingness. *Allow* yourself to contemplate your highest intentions.

Communication: I have noticed, during Intention Week, that many people hit the wall. They look at their lives and see unfulfilled dreams and empty intentions.   That happens. "Shift happens!"   And that's exactly what is happening. Whether or not you feel it, it's happening. You are shifting.

If you've come this far and have worked the program, you are shifting. You don't believe me?   It doesn't really matter whether or not you believe me. Do you believe yourself? Do you do what you say you're going to do? Have you followed the program? Have you put one of your intentions into action in the past few days? Are you expecting to complete it and demonstrate it by the next session? That's all that matters in this particular moment.

Do you understand what an intention is? Can you make one, and follow through, so that it doesn't wind up in the abyss of "just thinking?"

I think, therefore I am.

-166-

I intend, therefore I do!

- What have you decided to intend into being this week? What steps have you taken to manifest your intention? Write it down. Refer to it as you make your way through the week. Reinforce your desire to fulfill your intention. Become a man/woman of your **word...** especially in your relationship to yourself.

- How is your spiritual practice coming? Are you meditating more? Are you continuing with your morning journaling?

- For group work, share your intention with the others. Become accountable to the group for demonstrating your intention. Keep mindful of a time allotment. No cross-talk.

Accountability: Are you doing the work? If not, ask yourself why? Do you believe that you deserve to live life to the fullest as the highest expression of your True Self? You're the only one who can give you that experience.

Quotes from Boot Camp

"I cannot believe how may things I thought were intentions that were actually just hopes and plans and...I won't use the word I wanna use -, yes I will - just a bunch of crap. I still didn't use the word I wanted to use."

"I think I listen more to what other people intend for me."

"Without intentions I can avoid disappointment. That's what first came to me. I guess I'm going to have to look at that!"

"It seems like my intentions are based on what I 'think' I can accomplish. If I know I have control over something, then I know I can do it. It's the other things that seem out of reach so I don't intend anything about them."

Continue with this week's directives!

A meal is eaten one bite at a time, otherwise you might choke.

INTENTION

INTENTION

WEEK TWELVE

SELF-ESTEEM/RESPECT

WEEK TWELVE

Day One

Meditation: (Ten minute minimum)

"Before you speak, it is necessary for you to listen,
for God speaks in the silence of the heart."
Mother Teresa

Today, take a moment before you begin meditating to set the intention of listening. When you clearly set your intention, the Universe responds with action. *Allow* your mind to stay open. Listen, receive and discover your heart's intention.

Communication: This week, you were asked to pick an intention and see it through to its perfect conclusion. Were you able to accomplish this? What was the intention you chose? Was it something easy, simple, fun? Often, one of our biggest stumbling blocks is our creative way of putting things in categories. We think that curing a cold is easy while curing cancer is difficult. We decide that we have the ability to find a parking space when we need one ("good parking karma"), but we somehow cannot consider finding a job or the perfect mate as easy. We label some things as easy and others as difficult. The Truth is, it's all the same. Easy, hard, it's just a matter of perspective.

"There is no great and no small
to the soul that maketh all."
Ralph Waldo Emerson

This is one of my favorite quotes. How wonderful it is to

develop the mindset that whatever I decide to do is equally as doable as anything else. There's nothing to say that this thing is hard and something else is easier. I'm the only one who decides that. And I choose to decide whatever suits my needs. So, if I am contemplating a trip to Bali or a jog in the park, they are equally as doable. I just have to be clear of my intentions and let the Universe provide me with the details. Of course, it all comes from my willingness to act on my intention.

One Boot Camper shared that he felt like a hamster in a wheel. He runs and runs, trying to get where he's going, but he never gets anywhere other than where he is. Doesn't matter what the Intention is, he's standing still. He wanted something to help him break free from the wheel.

In acting, there's a thing called your "super objective." It's what a character wants overall from the story being told. This super objective is at the heart of every decision and behavior. It's the same with intention. At the heart of every specific intention is a super intention. If my overall objective in life is to succeed, then each of my specific intentions is going to be motivated by my super intention. Often what we find, however, is that much of our lives are being played out in conflict. I say I want happiness but my specific intentions don't match my super intention.

- What would you say is your super intention on a global scale, meaning your whole life picture?

- Look at your specific intention for the week. Does it compliment or clash with your super intention?

- Write down the history of how your intention manifested. Go back through the week and chronicle the steps you took to succeed at demonstrating your result. List the challenges, stumbling blocks (if any), and those times when it all just flowed.

- If, for some reason, you did not succeed, still chronicle your week's activities, regarding your intention as listed above.

- If you are in a group, share your thoughts. Keep mindful of a time allotment. No cross-talk.

Intention: This week's Intention/Directive is **Self-Esteem /Respect.**

> *"If you put a small value on yourself,*
> *rest assured that the world will not raise your price."*
> *Unknown*

On the heels of Intention comes Self-Esteem. One would imagine that if we knew the true depth of our Inner Being, our self-esteem would be concretized (set in stone – I just love that word).

What is your estimate of yourself? How deeply do you respect yourself? Most of us build our estimation of people out of what they accomplish. We can point to modern day figures who demand respect and attention. They have succeeded in ways that are admirable. We like what they have to say. We like what they do. We see in them what we would like to see in ourselves. They have confidence, charisma, success, and it is well-founded. I mean, just look at them.

When you see someone who is successful, it is right to conclude that they are clear on success. When you see someone who is happy, it is correct to conclude that they are clear on happiness. I am talking about people who we know are happy and successful, not those we think possess these qualities. Seeing someone on the cover of **People** magazine, smiling away with the new love of their life, doesn't mean a thing. Many times, it isn't even the love of their life. I know a lot of these people and what you read is rarely accurate. So, it's not celebrities that I'm referring to - it's the people in your life that you can point to and say, "he's happy," "she's successful."

What we are on the inside manifests itself on the outside in perfect proportion. If you want to know what you think about yourself, look around at your life. It will never fail to accurately exhibit a litmus test of your self-esteem. If you have a high **Respect** for yourself, it will show in how you live your life.

Respect is defined as, "esteem expressed toward a person." In the case of one's respect for self, therefore, it would seem that self-esteem is linked to **Respect** for the self. When I respect myself I make decisions differently. When I am rich with self-esteem, I walk confidently though each day knowing that my **Word** is the law of my life.

Attention: Pay attention this week to how you treat yourself. Pay attention as well to how you treat others. It's a mirror to what you think of yourself.

Directives for the Week: Continue with your morning journal.

  1. Keep an ongoing list of what your life looks like in

terms of self-esteem and respect. Have I built a life that is worthy of who I am? What things can I do in my present situation to build up and nurture my self-esteem? What things can I eliminate from my life that do not respect my self-worth? Make note of these things.

2. Do one thing for yourself each day that honors who you are. It could be a special meal, time alone, a walk on the beach, going through an old steamer trunk looking at pictures. Whatever it is, do it.

"We do not believe in ourselves until someone reveals that deep inside us is valuable, worth listening to, worthy of our trust, sacred to our touch. Once we believe in ourselves we can risk curiosity, wonder, spontaneous delight or any experience that reveals the human spirit."
e.e. cummings

The world will value you, as you do!

WEEK TWELVE

Day Two

Meditation: **I am worth it!**

When I look within, I see the light.
It illuminates the Truth that I am worth my highest
thought.
I continue on this journey of self-knowing,
recognizing that my life is limitless.

I AM WORTH IT!

Communication: Behind most failure is a belief of unworthiness. "I am worth it," although simple in thought, is a powerful measure of self-esteem. When you say this to yourself, what do you feel? Do you feel silly? Does it feel like the truth? Does it work for some things and not others?

"I am certainly worth a nice car, but a new career where
I call the shots seems out of reach."
Boot Camper

Often, in Boot Camp, I will hear people express frustration at not being able to move forward on certain issues. What we are taught to do is look at the facts and see what we can change, or what we can overcome. It is very easy to point the finger and see something external as the issue. "That" is in my way. The Truth is, YOU are in your way. We get to experience whatever we can consciously equal. In order to equal what we deserve, we must first know who we are. When I know that I am worthy of "the riches of the kingdom," as Jesus promised, then I equal the Truth and nothing can keep my good from me. It begins and ends with my self-esteem.

"Self esteem is the reputation we acquire with ourselves."
Nathaniel Branden

- Looking at your life, what do you conclude about your self-esteem? Do you treat yourself as though you are worth it? Are your decisions based on a healthy assessment of who you are?

- How do you feel when you are treating yourself to something nurturing?

- For group work, share your thoughts with one another. Keep mindful of a time allotment. No cross-talk.

Accountability:

1. Are you continuing to write in the mornings, keeping *Your Word* in the forefront of your mind?

2. Are you making lists of things in your life that are a direct result of your self-esteem and respect for yourself?

3. Have you taken time to do something for yourself each day that nurtures your self-esteem?

Remember: I AM WORTH IT!

*(Print out the affirmation, "I Am Worth It," and put it on a mirror, in your car, on your front door, somewhere that will allow you to remind yourself often.)

Quotes from Boot Camp

"It's so easy to think the best of someone else. Actually, it's not too hard to think the worst of them either. I do better with myself when I have something to judge me for."

"I don't think I've been too nice with myself."

"Wouldn't it be nice if everyone loved themselves? It would make life so much easier."

Continue with this week's directives!

YOU ARE WORTH IT!

SELF-ESTEEM/RESPECT

SELF-ESTEEM/RESPECT

WEEK THIRTEEN

COMMUNICATION

WEEK THIRTEEN

Day One

Meditation: (Ten minute minimum)

> *"This is love: to fly toward a secret sky,*
> *to cause a hundred veils to fall each moment.*
> *First to let go of life. Finally, to take a step without feet."*
> *Jalal ad-Din Rumi*

Take a step, during these next ten or so minutes, and allow yourself to drop whatever veils continue to cover your authentic self. Take a step without form into the silence of your mind. *Allow* yourself the pleasure of your true Self.

Communication: This week, you were asked to take time each day to honor yourself. Did you find things that strengthened your Life Force? Did you respect yourself enough to take time out of your busy schedule to refill your mind/body source?

> *Above all, be true to yourself.*
> *And if you cannot put your heart in it,*
> *take yourself out of it.*

How hard would it be for you to do only those things that made you happy? Does that sound like a fantasy world? Is it something you could believe in? Without a belief in the possibility of such a world, it will never come into being. Well, I do believe in such a world. And the initiating factor is to start, right here in this moment, to commit to things that make you happy. Conversely, you must begin to weed out those things that detract from your well being.

- Take a look at the list of things that contribute to your self-esteem and those that do not. Begin to target those things that no longer serve you. Make an informed, conscious list of those things that fill you up, make you happy, and infuse passion into your life.

- If you are in a group, make a commitment to those around you to continue staying on course, building your Energy Circle out of those things that reinforce healthy self-esteem and respect. Share those things with the group. Keep mindful of a time allotment. No cross-talk.

Intention: This week's Intention/Directive is **_Communication._**

> *"Tell me and I'll forget.*
> *Show me and I'll remember.*
> *Involve me and I'll understand."*
> *Confucius*

Since communication is an important part of Spiritual Boot Camp, it makes sense that we dedicate a week to what it means in the "bigger picture." How do we communicate to the world around us, to ourselves and to the impersonal law of cause and effect? What are we putting out there? Because whatever we are "putting out" is "coming back," whether we like it or not. That's how it works.

Communication is not just about the words we choose. It's smart to always be mindful of what words we decide to use in life, how we present ourselves and what we are attempting to accomplish with any communication. However, the initial thoughts, ideas, and desires behind the words are the substance of what we are truly communicating.

How many times have you had a conversation with someone, heard every word, and yet simultaneously heard the deafening sound of their "inner dialogue," the subtext to what was being said? We all know the saying, "actions speak louder than words." It's true. We communicate with action far more effectively than with words.

> *Sticks and stones may break my bones,*
> *but names will never hurt me.*

What do you think you communicate to the world on an ongoing basis? How are your words influenced by what you think, feel and ultimately believe?

Attention: Pay attention this week to how you communicate. Listen to the words you use, the catch phrases you utilize in order not to communicate or stall for time. Notice when you are saying things in direct conflict to what you are feeling.

Directives for the Week: Continue with your morning journal.

1. First thing each morning, check in to see how you are communicating with yourself. What are you telling yourself in those first few moments each day? Journal from this point of view.

2. Spend each day being mindful of how and what you are communicating to the world around you.

3. Make a list of all the catch phrases you use during the course of each day. Catch phrases are things that you use to avoid communication or stall for time to think. Often, these are things that we say out of habit and most of the time aren't even true.

"We are cups, constantly and quietly being filled.
The trick is, knowing how to tip ourselves over
and let the beautiful stuff out."
Ray Bradbury

Namaste' – The God in me salutes the God in you!

WEEK THIRTEEN

Day Two

Meditation: (Ten minute minimum)

> *"As fragrance abides in the flower*
> *As reflection is within the mirror,*
> *So does your Lord abide within you.*
> *Why search for him without?"*
> *Guru Nanak*

An important part of communication is the ability to hear. Take the next few moments to tune into the silence in such a way that you hear exactly what you need to hear.

Communication: Have you caught yourself shifting into catch phrases such as, "I don't know," "I know what you mean," "Why bother," and whatever else just comes out without thinking? It's maddening sometimes when you actually *allow* yourself to notice it. I realized, recently, that there were times when I would add an, "I don't know," in front of an answer just to take a moment to respond. How confident do you think it looks to respond to a question with "I don't know" and then give the answer? What am I communicating? Perhaps I want to come off as someone who isn't a know-it-all. Maybe I want people to know that I allow for opposing thought. Whatever the reason, I realized that it would be much better to use the correct words for what I'm thinking in the moment. "I don't know" needs to be reserved for when I don't know.

I remember when my twins were almost two. They would struggle to say what they wanted with words they had heard but perhaps didn't understand. One day my son was trying to say he wanted to go swimming and he kept saying, "Fool!" I thought he was a little young for sarcasm, so I wasn't feeling too insulted. Finally, after yelling "FOOL" for a few moments, he pulled me over to the window and pointed to the pool. When the wrong words get in the way, action is always best. Don't tell me! Show me! Good communication.

- What catch phrases have you caught?

- Looking around at those within your Energy Circle, do you think there's an authenticity to your communication?

- How well do you hear what you are communicating to yourself? Do you listen to what you have to say?

- For group work, share what "aha's" you've been having. Keep mindful of a time allotment. No cross-talk.

Accountability:

1. Have you continued to journal this week, focusing on the first thing you communicate to yourself in the morning?

2. Are you making a list of your catch phrases?

If not: what is that communicating to the creative Law of Cause and Effect?

Quotes from Boot Camp

"I occasionally say, 'You know what,' before I say something. It's like I'm asking myself to respond. That's weird and I never thought about it until now."

"Communication would be a lot easier if you just didn't have to communicate with other people."

"I feel like I communicate, just people don't always want to hear it."

"What's the healthy ratio between listening and speaking?"

Continue with this week's directives!

"Communication leads to community,
that is, to understanding, intimacy and mutual valuing."
Rollo May

COMMUNICATION

SPIRITUAL BOOT CAMP

COMMUNICATION

WEEK FOURTEEN

FEELINGS

WEEK FOURTEEN

Day One

Meditation: (Ten minute minimum)

> *When I look for You...my eyes delight.*
> *When I listen for You...there is music.*
> *When I hunger for You...the harvest is sweet.*
> *When I know You...I know myself.*

Allow your mind to empty of the relative facts. Sink deeply into the Absolute Truth of your Inner Being. It all begins with quieting the mind.

Communication: How do you communicate to the world? What comes out of your mouth most of the time? What goes into your head most of the time? Do people usually understand you? What percentage doesn't? How often do you have to repeat yourself? Are you someone who makes things clear, or do you leave things hanging? Are you okay with confusion? I know that sounds like a silly question. I mean, who would be okay with confusion? I think we spend a lot of time in confusion because we don't want to commit to being clear.

> *"I think I keep things nebulous so I have an escape route."*
> *Boot Camper*

I loved this quote from one of our Boot Campers. What we came to, in our session, was that every time communication is nebulous, the outcome matches it perfectly. At some point, someone is going to have to be clear. We only need escape routes when we find ourselves at risk. There's no risk to being truthful (with respect, always with respect).

- Did you find catch phrases that were stand-ins for actual thoughts and beliefs? What were they, and are you able to eliminate them?

- What came up with how you communicate to the world? Were you surprised, delighted, confused, annoyed............how do you communicate to the world?

- What do you communicate when you wake up? Have you been able to redirect anything you found to be limiting?

- Group work: Share your catch phrases, if you found any. Keep mindful of a time allotment. No cross-talk.

* This past week was a very full week. Check in to see if you did the required work. Stay mindful of the catch phrases used to detach from communication.

Intention: This week's Intention/Directive is **Feelings.**

*"I've learned that people will forget what you said,
people will forget what you did,
but people will never forget how you made them feel."*
Maya Angelou

There is a misconception that we feel based on what is going on around us. We often hear people ask us, "How does that make you feel?" We enter into long, often draining, conversations about our feelings in relation to this, or that, or any number of things we blame for our feelings. Years and years of therapy can be spent in trying to get to the feelings. But I think we might do better to consciously decide what we feel in the first place and then move forward from there.

A bunch of us went to see a movie this past holiday season. I won't name the movie, but suffice to say that it was a musical that was highly anticipated. In the dark of the room, we all experienced the same screen, the same dialogue, the same actors singing the same songs. We were all at the "same" movie. When we came out you would have thought the skies had opened and we were experiencing a modern day "Tower of Babel." I was trying to explain how a certain part brought tears to my eyes, when one of our group started laughing. He said that the only tears that came to his eyes were from the air hitting his tear ducts - his eyes had been popped open so wide from his disbelief of how anyone could take a perfectly good stage musical and destroy it like that. WOW! What happened? Same movie, different people.

Feelings come from what someone brings to the party, not from the party itself.

What I have noticed, in my life, is that every time I blame something or someone for making me feel a certain way, I wind up with more of the same feeling and less of who I am. In the end, I am responsible for what I feel. <u>When I feel good, I own it.</u> <u>When I feel bad, I change it.</u> It's that simple.

Attention: This week, pay attention to how you feel in any given situation. Notice your proclivity to "pinning" it on something or someone other than yourself. Pay attention to what you bring to the party. You're there; you might as well enjoy it.

Directives for the Week: Continue with your morning journal.

1. First thing each morning, ask yourself, "How do I feel?" Decide, in the moment, if this is good or bad. Recognize that you can go with the "flow" or redirect the current. Your choice!

2. Ask yourself throughout the day, "What am I feeling?" Trace your feelings back to your own thoughts/beliefs. Don't judge yourself or your feelings. Notice them, own them and take charge of them.

3. At the end of each day, in a very short sentence, capsulate your feelings experience.

"A man sooner or later discovers
that he is the master-gardener of his soul,
the director of his life."
James Allen

Feel good – it's who you are!

WEEK FOURTEEN

Day Two

Meditation: (Ten minute minimum)

Allow the following words to take you into your silence.

> *"Oh, for a tongue to express the Wonders*
> *which the thought reveals!*
> *Oh, for some Word to comprehend*
> *the boundless idea!*
> *Would that some voice were sweet enough*
> *to sound the harmony of Life.*
> *But Within, in that vast realm of thought*
> *where the Soul meets God,*
> *the Spirit knows.*
> *I will listen to that voice and it will tell me*
> *of Life, of Love and Unity."*
> Ernest Holmes

Communication: How have you been feeling? Are you noticing that your feelings are actually a result of how you approach life? We can decide how we're going to feel in any given situation, not by forcing ourselves to feel a certain way, but by strengthening our beliefs in such a way that we orchestrate the symphony that is our life.

If I know that I am always going to see the good in any situation, then my feelings are filtered through that belief. If I know that there is evil lurking out there to "get me," then my feelings will go the road before me and jump out at me like a ghoul in a horror flick. As much as I like **Psycho**, I don't want to shower in that house.

*"The trick is in what one emphasizes.
We either make ourselves miserable, or we make
ourselves happy.
The amount of work is the same."*
Carlos Castaneda

- Look at what you have written, thus far, about your feelings. Is there a pattern?

- Have you been able to trace your feelings back to a belief and restructure it to create the feelings you want?

- For group work, talk about the communication of the Boot Camp thus far. Keep mindful of a time allotment. No cross-talk.

Accountability:

1. Are you taking the morning time necessary to center your mind and focus your day?

2. Are you checking in at night with the day's feelings?

3. Have you begun to take charge of your mind?

How do you feel about where you are in this Boot Camp? Trace it back.

Quotes from Boot Camp

"You mean I can't blame my mother anymore? That doesn't feel right. I'm joking, of course. Sort of."

"I've excavated this gnawing 'feeling' that things just

might not work out for me. I seem to bring it to every party."

"My wife told me that I don't like 'feeling' things. But I think I just don't like feeling 'bad' things."

Continue with this week's directives!

**"It's a new dawn, it's a new day, it's a new life...
FEELING GOOD!"
Leslie Bricusse**

FEELINGS

_____

_____

_____

_____

_____

_____

_____

_____

_____

_____

_____

_____

_____

_____

_____

_____

_____

_____

_____

_____

_____

_____

FEELINGS

_____

_____

_____

_____

_____

_____

_____

_____

_____

_____

_____

_____

_____

_____

_____

_____

_____

_____

_____

_____

_____

_____

_____

_____

WEEK FIFTEEN

JUDGMENT

WEEK FIFTEEN

Day One

Meditation: (Ten minute minimum)

Allow your thoughts to slip away. In their place, ask the following question:

What do I need to know?

As you enter this sacred time you have reserved for yourself, continue to empty your mind by suggesting the question:

What do I need to know?

Allow yourself to know something new.

Communication: "Feelings Week" is always an interesting time for Boot Campers. Waking up and asking ourselves, "How do I feel?" requires a certain amount of willingness to be honest and daring. There can be an underlying sense of "doom" in one's unconscious mind that, over time, becomes second nature. What happens then is that all of life is filtered through this "veil" and the picture is always out of focus. And there are many veils to choose from.

When you first wake up in the morning is the perfect time to check in and see, "How do I feel?" One Boot Camper noticed that his "feeling" was somehow linked to the weather. He recognized that, if it was a sunny, warm morning, he could pop right out of bed and jump into his day. If it were cold and damp, he would creak off the mattress, bones stiff and brittle, and slowly get the day going. It had nothing to do with health, he assured me. It was all mental. So he started jumping out of bed in the morning, regardless of the weather. It worked. He took charge of his feelings.

There are many reasons for us to feel the way we feel. In order to understand our feelings, we need to be *aware* of what we feel and why, and *active* in our approach to take control. When we actively take control of our feelings, we begin to see that we are at choice. I can choose to *feel good* in the face of anything. Dr. Tom Costa, the founding pastor of the Palm Desert Center for Spiritual Living, in a brilliant moment of prayer, suggested that we add these words to our affirmations:

NO MATTER WHAT!

No matter what I am feeling, I will not give up my right to choose. *No matter what* is going on in my life, I will not forget who I am. *No matter what* seems to be standing in my way, I will always remember that there is *good* for me to have.

I cannot tell you how often I use this phrase in my life. Whenever I start to feel overwhelmed or uncertain, I remember who I am, what I am capable of and I look straight into the fire and claim, *NO MATTER WHAT*. Try it, it works.

- Look at what you wrote each night this week. What was your "feelings" journey like? Did you recognize any "veils?" Have you stripped them away?

- Did you notice yourself pinning your feelings on people and situations outside of yourself?

Were you able to redirect the energy to a place where the feelings were transformed?

- Group work: Be fearless in sharing your feelings from the week. Keep mindful of a time allotment. No cross-talk.

Intention: The Intention/Directive for this week is ***Judgment.***

> *"Everything that irritates us about others can lead us to an understanding of ourselves."*
> Carl Jung

This week is all about judgment. Are you a judgmental person? Do you get caught up with people and situations that are "just wrong?" Does your opinion turn to a judgment in the spark of an instant? How are you when it comes to judging yourself? Are you your worst critic? What exactly is judgment?

For our work this week, judgment is that part of opinion that turns ugly. When there is heat around an opinion, there is something more at play. When a situation suddenly becomes personal, we are sinking into judgment. And it's not pretty. It's one thing to send back an entrée in a restaurant. It's another thing altogether to curse the chef for treating you so poorly, shove the table over and storm out the front door. I doubt the chef even knows who you are.

An informed opinion leads us to making clear decisions. A reactive judgment, based on relative facts, colors our thoughts and most of the time only leads to heartburn.

"If you judge people, you have no time to love them."
Mother Teresa

Recognizing when we are in judgment and when we are in right relation to our opinions is a road to freedom. Ridding ourselves of this time-consuming preoccupation will be a relief.

Attention: This week, pay attention to your inner and outer dialogue. Notice when you are standing in judgment of someone or something. Be very attentive to what your inner dialogue produces in terms of self-judgment.

Directives for the Week: Continue with your morning journal.

1. In each instance, when you catch yourself being judgmental, take the time to turn it around. See through the veil of judgment and impersonalize the facts. If you feel heat, cool yourself down. Make it an intention for the week to eradicate judgment from your life.

2. Each evening, before you go to bed, rate yourself on a scale of one to ten, "was I judgmental today?"

"Love has no opposite. Duality is man-made."
Ernest Holmes

WEEK FIFTEEN

Day Two

Meditation: (Ten minute minimum)

For that place in me
Where there is only light
For that voice in me
Where there is only Truth
For that part of me
Where there is only One

Take a moment to repeat this quote a few times. Allow the words to become your Reality. As the relative world slips away, drift into the Absolute, where you find your *place*, your *voice* and your *Oneness* with God.

Communication: Each week has been designed to release those things that no longer serve us and to cultivate a "Spiritual Practice" that aligns us with our highest good. Judgment week is no exception. There are things that take us down a path of negative results. Being judgmental is one of those paths. One Boot Camper said that getting rid of her judgmental attitude reminded her of the time she fell into a row of cactus. Every time she thought she'd pulled out all of the thorns, she would find another. As painful as it was to pull the suckers, they had to come out. Otherwise there would have been an infection.

"Spiritual progress is like detoxification.
Things have to come up in order to be released.
Once we have asked to be healed,

then our unhealed places are forced to the surface."
Marianne Williamson

For the past couple of days, you've been willing to look at what's been coming up in terms of being judgmental.

- What have you found? How have you been rating yourself? What does it bring up for you? Can you distinguish between opinion and judgment?

- How does it feel when you impersonalize the facts? Does it become easier to let go of the judgment? Are you more comfortable with opinions, detaching them from judgment?

- For group work, share your experience, thus far, with becoming *aware* of judgment and how it plays out in your life. Keep mindful of a time allotment. No cross-talk.

Accountability:

1. Are you taking time to meditate before each session?

2. Are you fearlessly patrolling your mind for moments when you step into judgment? Are you turning it around or just letting it continue?

Quotes from Boot Camp

"When something isn't a duck, calling it a duck doesn't make it a duck. It just makes me stupid!"

"Opinion vs. judgment, that is the question."

"It's hard not to judge people. They give you so much to work with."

"This week should've come earlier. I need a lot of time to work with judgment. It's something I do very well."

"I've noticed this week that when I catch myself judging someone, stop and rethink it, I actually feel better. Who knew?"

Continue with this week's directives!

"Judgments prevent us from seeing the good that lies beyond appearances."
Wayne Dyer

JUDGMENT

JUDGMENT

WEEK SIXTEEN

ACCOUNTABILITY

WEEK SIXTEEN

Day One

Meditation: (Ten minute minimum)

If you're ready to take your life in a new direction, if you're ready to take control of your mind and create a tomorrow that seems out of reach, if you're ready to put some MENTAL SWEAT into your Spiritual/Mental creative muscle, then this is for you.

In the final week of Boot Camp, *allow* yourself to reflect on why you began this journey. Use these operative words to propel you into your "silence."

"A – New – Direction"
"A – New – Me"

Communication: You have made it all the way through to week sixteen of Spiritual Boot Camp. How does it feel? Have you created a network of tools to keep you mentally fit? In terms of judgment, where have you landed on your score chart? Do you know the difference between opinion and judgment? Can you recognize when the "heat" steps in and drags you down into that dark judgmental abyss?

The funny thing about judgment is that it is often confused for conversation. We are so quick to judge others that it becomes a way of life for some people. Have you ever been dragged into a conversation only to find yourself surrounded by judgmental people, all wanting you to agree with their assessment of someone or something? It's like a drug. You have to have the internal strength to "just say no." Social "dishing," although an unfortunately acceptable part of society, does not move you forward on your spiritual path.

So how did you do?

- Were you aware when you were being judgmental? That's the start, being aware. From awareness comes opportunity to step into action. Were you able to impersonalize the facts and turn them around? Was there a willingness to be less judgmental?

- Were you clear on when you were dealing with opinion and when you stepped into judgment? How did they feel different? What signs were you looking for to distinguish them, one from the other?

- How did you rate on your chart? Are you committed to lowering your numbers, if they are higher than you would want? A good number is **zero**. No, I'm not kidding.

- Group work: Share your week with judgment. Be scorchingly honest, there's only one session left. Keep mindful of a time allotment. No cross-talk.

Intention: This week's Intention/Directive is ***Accountability.***

I remember reading about an interesting tradition of the ancient Romans. Whenever one of their engineers constructed an arch, as the capstone was hoisted into place, the engineer assumed accountability for his work in the most profound way possible: he stood under the arch.

Are you willing to stand under the arch of your creation? For the past sixteen weeks, you have *allowed* yourself to know yourself. You have fearlessly taken a look at things in your life, qualities of existence, character traits, beliefs, and annoying habits. You have put your life under a microscope and examined it day-by-day, moment-by-moment, nuance-by-nuance. In a sense, you have scientifically dissected your personal character and replaced old, archaic, rusty tools with new ones. You have become the creator of your experience. No longer the "reactive" bystander, you are now the Absolute Word in your own life.

I remember when I first heard the saying, "Change your thinking, change your life!" I was instantly hooked. It all made sense to me, in that moment, that my life was playing itself out exactly as I was orchestrating it. I just didn't know I was doing it. Once we find out that we are always at "choice," we become responsible for the lives we live. <u>Being *accountable* is putting your Word into action.</u> You get to decide! You get to choose! You get to create! How great is that?

> *"Thought is the instrument of Mind.*
> *New thoughts create new conditions."*
> *Ernest Holmes*

It's up to you to create *new thoughts*. You are at the threshold of a new awareness. Hold yourself *accountable* to continue the work you have started. Be true to your word. Find new words. Live them! Renew them! Revive them! It's all up to you.

Attention: During the next few days, before the final

session, read over your journal. *Allow* the journey of words, ideas and feelings to wash over you with a sense of freedom, ease and accomplishment. Recognize yourself on the page, mindful of who you are in this moment.

Your Journey

The Word
Complaining
Expectations
Belief
Present
Patience
Listen/Hear/Resolve
Boundaries/Priorities
Life Force
Perfectionism
Intention
Self-Esteem
Communication
Feelings
Judgment
Accountability

Directives for the Week: Continue with your morning journal. How does it feel reaching the conclusion of Boot Camp?

This week, you have one specific directive: Write out a "Spiritual Resume." Apply for the job of **God**. In your own words and style, communicate to the world why you are right for this job and what skills you have to fulfill the requirements.

This has always been my favorite part of Spiritual Boot

Camp. There are as many ways to accomplish this task as there are people. One person came in and presented his Spiritual Resume as an original song. Another did a rap that blew us all away. Others wrote formal resumes, comical resumes, and traditional and not so traditional renderings. There is no wrong way to create your Spiritual Resume other than to not do it.

> *"Every individual has a place to fill in the world,*
> *and is important, in some respect,*
> *whether he chooses to be so or not."*
> Nathaniel Hawthorne

Quotes from Boot Camp

"If I get the job as God, things are sure gonna change around here."

"I have to say that I thought I'd be a lot more uncomfortable with the idea of being God than I am. I AM! Why not?"

"Usually I pad my resume but somehow that doesn't seem right here."

"I couldn't get the image of George Burns out of my head. Then it was Morgan Freeman. I'm working my way to me."

Continue with this week's directives!

It's time for you to show the world who you are.

WEEK SIXTEEN

Final Day

Meditation: Try meditating today without a time limit. Allow yourself the time to slow down. Whatever works for you today, do it. You're in charge. It's your intention. It's whatever you want. Let these words of Kathryn Skatula inform you in some way. Be gentle with your mind.

When a smile touches our core,
When the eyes connect inside the deepest trust,
When the forest stills us to peace,
When the music moves us to rapture,
When glee paralyzes us into dizzying laughter,
When passion removes the fear of the dance,
When we really love...
We are one with the angels.

Communication: In the spirit of **So You Think You Can Dance**, we take you to **So You Think You Are God**. All of the contestants have worked very hard to get to where they are, and to exhibit the talents they possess, with such craft and skill they make it look easy.   In the interview process, they all told us how they just knew that they were the next "God."   Some of them were clearly pumping themselves up due to a lack of confidence or some such nonsense. Others were just certain that they would land in the Top Ten. And some still weren't sure but were willing to give it their best shot.

In this particular show, what the contestant doesn't know is that there really isn't a competition. There will never be a Number One. The "One" title is a conglomerate of the sum total of all of its contestants. Each one is needed to provide their "spin" on the Universal Beat. **So You Think You Can Dance** works because we witness the magnificence of Spirit flowing out of each unique player. Interestingly enough, the one who ultimately "wins" (and I use that term in the relative world only) will be the one who, on some level, has tapped into his or her God-ness.

- How does it feel stepping into your Spiritual Power?

- Are you willing to find God within your every thought?

- Can you own the Truth that you are the co-creator of your life?

- Will you remain *accountable* for your actions, remembering that your future is in your own hands?

- Is your *Word* now part of who you are?

Group Work: If you are doing Spiritual Boot Camp in a group, on this final day, each will read his or her Spiritual Resume out loud. Once everyone has had an opportunity to read, go around the room again and share final thoughts. Cross-talk is permitted, provided it holds the integrity and highest consciousness of the room.

Congratulations! You have concluded Spiritual Boot Camp!

I _____ have completed 16 weeks of Spiritual Boot Camp. I hereby make a commitment to myself to adhere to the lessons I have learned. I recognize the Truth that within me is the mental muscle to create greatness. I promise myself to continue my Spiritual Practice by using the tools that work for me, releasing what doesn't work and focusing my attention on my "chosen" intentions.

> *"There is good for me, and I ought to have it!"*
> *Emma Curtis Hopkins*

I say YES to this! I accept my good! I expect my good! I AM my good!

Signed: _____

Date: _____

ACCOUNTABILITY

_____

_____

_____

_____

_____

_____

_____

_____

_____

_____

_____

_____

_____

_____

_____

_____

_____

_____

_____

_____

_____

_____

_____

ACCOUNTABILITY

_____

_____

_____

_____

_____

_____

_____

_____

_____

_____

_____

_____

_____

_____

_____

_____

_____

_____

_____

_____

_____

_____

_____

_____

_____

WHAT NEXT?

After writing this book, I was faced with the final task of writing a "conclusion." I noticed, as I sat down to write, that I was balking at the idea of there even being a conclusion. In my mind, there is always more. We live in an Infinite Universe that is capable of unlimited creative expression, placing us in the midst of a vast sea of knowledge, understanding and adventure. There is no finish line, just a magnificent journey. When we complete one thing, we are merely ready for the *Next*. So I guess the logical question is, what's next?

That question can be answered in as many ways as there are grains of sand on a beach. We are pure potentiality ready to explore the horizons of our own individual mind. We are co-creators with The Creator. We can do whatever we *decide* to do. We can achieve whatever *intention* we choose to live. We can create whatever we *believe* we can accomplish. It is up to each of us to take what we *know* and put it to use. And so, we do.

I honor you for taking this spiritual journey. I honor each and every blessed journey that will follow. I honor where you are in this moment, each moment that brought you to this point, and where you will travel as you move forward. I recognize the greatness in you, recognizing the greatness in me, recognizing the Truth that we are forever One. *Namaste'!*

ACKNOWLEGEMENTS

"If the only prayer you said in your whole life was, 'thank you,' that would suffice."
Meister Eckhart

I want to thank my Board of Trustees at The NoHo Arts Center for New Thought, past and present, who have called me forth to be a better man, a stronger leader and a passionate visionary. Through your love, support and encouragement, I continue to "Live Life to the Fullest."

I especially want to thank Suzanne Benoit for taking the time to "nudge" me along, through it all and "no matter what." Your skills as an editor, but more importantly, your skills as a friend truly made this book come to life.

Special thanks also to Cheryl Fluehr, my "life" editor, for your wisdom and support. To Barbara Shane, for always taking any challenge by the horns and leading by example, and to Jonathan Zenz, my right arm, for being the pure Spirit you are.

To Dr. Eric Butterworth, my first teacher of the New Thought Principles and to Dr. David J. Walker, my teacher, my mentor and my "linoleum." To Leslie Hinton, for designing such a beautiful book cover, yes, but for designing such a loving friendship even more. To Rob Arbogast, for taking such a flattering picture of me and to Tom Lasley for your "artistic invention."

A special word must be said for Rita Andriello, who has assisted me through sixty-four weeks of Boot Camp unfailingly. Your love, energy, commitment and leadership contribute to this book in ways impossible to communicate. Thank you! And to Lynn Klein, who has facilitated in my absence, for your clarity, integrity and beauty through and through. You are always there, and I am eternally grateful.

To all the Boot Campers, who have shared their desires, intentions, passions, challenges, who have fearlessly taken the journey within and faced the Truth, wrestled with the relatives and crossed the finish line only to find a new frontier waiting to be explored. Thank you for trusting me and for trusting yourself.

And last, and certainly most of all, to the man who keeps all of my dreams clearly in view at all times, tirelessly gives of himself to make them all come true, and shares all aspects of my life with me - my soul mate, my partner, my teacher, my confidant and my best friend, Kevin Bailey. *"With every sunrise, I love you more."*